SOCIAL SKILLS FOR TEENS DECODED

MASTER COMMUNICATION AND EMOTIONAL INTELLIGENCE - ENHANCE ONLINE SAFETY, BUILD HEALTHY RELATIONSHIPS, AND BOOST SOCIAL CONFIDENCE

YUDELKIS MURRAY

TABLE OF CONTENTS

INTRODUCTION

At age 15, Zoe dreaded walking the halls of her high school. She felt invisible as her peers laughed and talked in their close-knit friend groups while she quietly made her way from class to class. Group projects were torturous, and she avoided speaking up even when she had worthy ideas to contribute. Her  social anxiety was stifling her confidence and sense of belonging. Zoe often chose to eat lunch alone rather than face potential rejection from the chatter-filled cafeteria tables around her. She yearned for true connection but felt trapped inside her shyness.

It was in her sophomore year when Zoe discovered her school's debate club. Though apprehensive at first, she took a chance and joined, comforted by the structure and guidance it provided. As she learned effective communication techniques and constructive critique, she slowly emerged from her shell. The weekly debates boosted her public speaking skills and taught her how to craft persuasive arguments. She also realized everyone got nervous speaking in front of others, helping her overcome her fear of judgment. Fast forward a year later and Zoe was now the club president, leading meetings with poise and assurance she never thought possible. Through determination and the skills she acquired, she transformed her social abilities and unearthed a confident leader within.

Zoe's story is one of courage and growth but also mastery over the complex arena of social skills. For most teenagers like her, navigating the ever-evolving social landscape of peers, school, family, and the digital world can be overwhelming and frustrating. The unwritten rules of teen social hierarchies are often perplexing, the influence of social media is inescapable, and the risk of rejection feels heightened. Some common struggles teens face are difficulty initiating or holding conversations, fear of judgment, the pressure to fit in, and managing conflict and rejection. Without strong social skills, teens often feel isolated and unable to connect genuinely with others or advocate for themselves. Their friendships and even mental health may suffer as a result.

In this comprehensive guide, I will empower you to decode the social intricacies of adolescence and provide actionable strategies to communicate effectively, expand your network, stand up to peer pressure, resolve disagreements, influence peers, and even leverage social media productively. Over 10 chapters, we will cover self-awareness, masterful communication across mediums, conflict management, leadership, empathy, understanding romantic relationships, and much more. This book will equip you to navigate complex social terrain with compassion and emotional intelligence.

With engaging case studies and step-by-step templates personalized for today's teenage challenges, this book will be your hands-on manual to social success. You will discover how best to articulate your voice, make real connections online and offline, learn from mistakes, and establish boundaries. While social mastery requires practice, this evidence-based guide will demonstrate exactly how to put key principles into action in family, friend, academic, and professional settings. After absorbing the book's lessons, you will have a tool kit of techniques tailored to thrive socially no matter the scenario.

By the final chapter, the confidence and skills you will have mastered will empower you to navigate high school and beyond with an unshakable sense of self-assurance. You will not only overcome the paralyzing social stress faced by many teens but also tap into reservoirs of previously untapped potential. With the strategies revealed in the coming pages, you too can build an expansive social circle, make a real impact through advocacy, and stand firmly in what you believe. This book will set you up for positive social experiences now and the poise to interact fluidly in college or workplace settings.

The tools are at your fingertips; turn the page to begin your life-changing journey toward social brilliance and leadership.

1

THE SOCIAL LANDSCAPE OF TODAY'S TEENS

"Children are the living messages we send to a time we will not see."

— NIEL POSTMAN

This quote by Neil Postman reflects the idea that the social landscape of today's teens is shaped by past messages and influences, highlighting the importance of understanding and guiding young people in the digital age.

At 14, Michael hated walking the school halls. He felt invisible as friends laughed together about weekend plans. Group projects were torture even when he had good ideas. His quietness set in when peers seemed to talk so easily. He wanted to disappear rather than risk rejection. Without that social component, Michael's confidence sank.

However, in 10th grade, Michael found an online gaming group and created a new side of himself. At first, he simply played without chatting much, feeling too awkward to interact more. Slowly though, as his strategy skills shone, he took baby steps out of his nerdy shell to lead missions. His gamer friends couldn't tell shyness plagued him offline.

Two years later, he was moderating lively forum debates with a confidence unthinkable before finding this community aligned with his passion. Bit by bit, he succeeded in putting himself out there to connect in the digital world.

However, when Michael imagined approaching his high school lunch squad to make IRL friends, panic returned quickly. Real teenage social life seemed like an unsolvable maze of unspoken cliques and rules. Why did his skills for making online pals escape him offscreen?

Lots of teens feel baffled by the evolving social codes that dictate their school days and nights. Starting convos, constant fear of mocking by the popular kids, decoding confusing group chat drama —it's non-stop. No rule book exists for navigating these intricate peer webs to find deeper bonds or even just survive lunch! But by starting to understand social skills and learning to refine your own, you can make your journey just a little bit easier.

UNDERSTANDING YOUR SOCIAL ENVIRONMENT

Navigating complex social landscapes is a huge challenge for many teenagers. To successfully traverse the maze of unwritten societal norms, subtle nonverbal cues, and ever-evolving peer interests, you must first understand the social environment itself.

In this section, we'll dive deeper into the external worlds you must operate within daily. These worlds shape your communication patterns, self-concept, and by extension, life path. We'll explore the digital spaces that captivate adolescent attention today, including social media's double-edged impacts. We'll demystify academic institutions and extracurriculars as social opportunity platforms that can also be rife with judgment pressures. Finally, we look at how your family's influence can often be overlooked but leaves a relational blueprint you carry with you throughout your life.

By illuminating these contextual forces, we'll empower you to appraise your social environments through a more informed, nuanced lens. Only once you grasp the natural sociological ecosystems that affect your daily life can you strategize to maximize the social upsides and reduce the pain points. Consider this section an insider's field guide into teenage society's driving forces, from screen culture and peer microcosms to role modeling by siblings and adults. Internalizing the social meta-patterns that silently orchestrate your life is the first step to choosing how you wish to interact with them on your own confident terms. Let's pull back the curtain.

The Digital Age and Social Interaction

The prominence of social media and smartphones has fundamentally reshaped how teenagers socialize today. With 24-7 connectivity and platforms allowing instant sharing of photos, videos, and messages, digital technology has profoundly impacted communication norms and behaviors.

The pull toward digital interaction over face-to-face communication is strong because devices provide constant access to peer groups and validation via likes and comments. Did you know that most teens spend an average of over seven hours a day on screens, limiting crucial in-person encounters that build empathy and allow reading of nonverbal cues (Solis, 2007)? This can impair the development of emotional intelligence.

Additionally, the anonymity and detachment of digital communication enable harassment, including bullying and explicit content sharing without seeing the human impact, which most teenagers are still learning to consider. The screens between individuals seem to limit sympathy.

Social media also heightens peer comparison and pressures to present perfected images of beauty, success, and popularity online. This can affect your self-esteem, as real life fails to match the projected appearances. Teens craving social approval often portray their best possible selves rather than their real personalities. This curation threatens authenticity in relationships.

Moreover, always-on networking provides teenagers with little time for self-reflection away from constant peer input. Practicing mindfulness, offline hobbies, and self-awareness is key to balancing technology's saturation of daily life.

With personal data transparency, you must also recognize that comments, photos, and posts leave lasting digital footprints. In a hyperconnected world, online reputations deeply influence college admission and job opportunities. So, creating a positive digital footprint requires understanding and care.

Of course, with all the access and anonymity digital spaces allow, cyberbullying and the circulation of inappropriate photos are serious pitfalls you must learn to navigate safely. Protecting your personal privacy and digital well-being means you need to understand that technology comes with benefits as well as risks.

The key here is balance. Teens can benefit immensely from online access to others but need to seek guidance on using technology constructively rather than compulsively. When used positively, digital platforms enhance organizing, networking, and staying connected. With proper etiquette on liking, commenting, and sharing, social technologies can facilitate rather than replace interpersonal bonds. Maintaining that healthy equilibrium between screens and genuine human connection is the modern challenge you face.

School and Extracurriculars as Social Arenas

Academic environments and extracurricular activities provide invaluable opportunities for you to expand your social circles, develop new skills, and unwind through organized hobbies. However, these settings also introduce complex group dynamics to navigate.

Juggling intensive academic workloads from classes and college applications can compete heavily with your desire for a vibrant social life. Prioritizing your time is essential, but it can be difficult with the mounting pressures to perform academically. Understanding this tug-of-war is key for you, your parents, and your teachers.

As you've surely noticed, within classrooms and schools, there are distinct social hierarchies, complete with "unpopular" and "cool" crowds. Where one sits in the cafeteria carries weight in the social strata. You can feel the pressure to fit in among certain peers but need guidance on inclusivity over clique-ishness.

Additionally, interest clubs, athletic teams, and niche friend groups can have unique subcultures with unwritten norms. While extracurriculars connect teens who share common interests, each group bears hallmark rituals, fashion tastes, and internal politics that form a complex social microcosm to navigate.

Leadership roles within clubs and teams can provide you with opportunities to practice invaluable skills such as time management, public speaking, accountability, conflict resolution, and organizational vision. These roles can build confidence while allowing low-stakes leadership exposure.

Finally, conferences, academic competitions, and sporting events open access to expanding your social connections to teens from other schools and backgrounds. These events can give you diverse perspectives and contrast the usual high school bubble, which can help to spur maturity. They also facilitate networking opportunities that can be useful to you professionally in the future.

In navigating these enriching but demanding environments, you must intentionally maximize social advantages while minimizing the potential stresses. Seeking diverse friends beyond the obvious cliques, trying multiple activities that align with your interests rather than just one social bubble, and prioritizing genuine connections amidst packed schedules are all constructive strategies to aim for. The skills you build by managing this balancing act will prove invaluable for your future work life, too.

The Family Unit and Social Development

Your family environment plays a profound role in shaping your communication abilities, emotional intelligence, and social skills from childhood through adolescence. As your first and most intimate social sphere, your home and family dynamics establish the blueprint for interpersonal relating that you will often continue to emulate.

Early childhood attachments, conversations, play, and even conflict management examples with caregivers constitute the foundational relational templates you unconsciously reference. The social mirroring you absorb in those highly impressionable young years leaves lasting imprints.

When your family maintains open communication channels, they enable you to express your sometimes swirling emotions and feel genuinely understood by family members. This fosters trust and creates a safe haven for authentic connection. You can then recreate these vulnerability-baring patterns among friends.

In addition to family communication, healthy sibling relationships built on mutual understanding, compromise, playfulness, and affection can provide you with invaluable relationship practice opportunities that can help create smooth peer interactions later. Learning how to give and take starts at home.

Alternately, unresolved family conflicts, domestic tensions, or poor home communication coping mechanisms can often spill over, manifesting for adolescents as anti-social behaviors, social anxiety, or aggression with peers and authority figures outside the home. It is an unfortunate fact that internal distress can be mirrored externally.

Every day, teenagers closely observe and subconsciously adopt conflict moderation approaches, phrasing of advice, conversational mannerisms, inside jokes, and even slang terms from parents and older sibling figures. This familial modeling never stops, even during your teenage years when peer influences spike in dominance.

While peers undoubtedly sway your external social roles, the truly foundational impact still lies with the family emotional bonds nurtured since childhood. Assessing their own upbringing can help your parents evolve increasingly constructive communication patterns and model ideal social skills that support developmental health overall.

THE ROLE OF PERSONALITY IN SOCIAL INTERACTIONS

While the external social environments you and most teenagers navigate undoubtedly influence behaviors, the inner landscape of your personality shapes your individual experience just as much. Your innate temperament drives how you perceive situations and determines the very lens through which you interpret social cues. Who you are internally colors all you encounter externally.

This section will look at the relationship between personality and social skills. We'll discover the three prevailing teen personality archetypes—introverts, extroverts, and ambiverts—and unpack how each social orientation carries distinct communication patterns, preferences, and even blind spots requiring self-awareness. You'll then be guided through an assessment to identify your social styles.

The goal is to embrace your uniqueness rather than force rigid conformity to standards that don't align with who you are. Growth depends not on drastic personality overhauls but on nurturing your natural strengths while acknowledging the areas that need improvement. With maturity comes recognizing that social skills require adapting your communication approaches to each circumstance and audience. It is not a one-size-fits-all formula.

Just as crucially, appreciating personality diversity in your peers allows you to interact more empathetically across groups. As social beings, we must each understand diverse social orientations to nurture cohesion, not division. We can look inward to expand outward in a meaningful way.

Introverts, Extroverts, and Ambiverts

Personality profoundly impacts your social preferences and communication style. While there is, of course, individual variation within these labels, three personality types help illustrate the most common tendencies:

- Introverts feel more at ease and recharged in quiet settings with meaningful one-on-one interactions rather than constant chit-chat and mingling with large crowds. They prefer listening over dominating conversations and focused depth over breadth in relationships. Structure enables introverts to prepare mentally for socializing.
- Extroverts, conversely, feel energized and in their element when actively engaging with others in dynamic group scenarios, such as at parties or in collaborative projects. They think out loud while articulating in fast-paced conversations. Extroverts enjoy spotlight moments when they can express themselves creatively and feed off audience reactions.
- Ambiverts have both introverted and extroverted qualities, intuitively adjusting their social approach based on the context and mood. Blending reflective and gregarious modes, they can adopt the characteristics of both introverts and extroverts like social chameleons. Ambiverts recognize

that the energy they must expend socially depends on the circumstance.

Understanding these differences in personality and sociability can help you better understand your inclinations. Without judgment, introverts should recognize their need for solo downtime to recharge batteries drained by excessive stimulation. Extroverts, however, may need to learn to appreciate solo time rather than crave perpetual engagement. Ultimately, personality awareness enables you to play to your innate social strengths while addressing weaknesses through intentional personal growth in areas such as public speaking confidence.

Self-Assessment: Identifying Your Social Style

Determining where you fall on the introvert-extrovert spectrum requires honest self-reflection in assessing your social tendencies. Ask yourself:

- Do I feel energized or drained after heavy social interactions? Introverts may crave solitary downtime to recharge afterward.
- Do I prefer deep one-on-one conversations or casual chatting amongst groups? Extroverts thrive on always mingling.
- Do I function better solo or bounce ideas off others when decision-making? Collaborative work suits extroverts.
- In groups, am I the quiet observer, vocal leader, or flexible participant depending on comfort levels? Ambiverts morph roles.
- Additionally, examine your behavior after social gatherings. Did you relax alone or continue engaging

others? Did you network proactively or rely on friends to make connections?

Keep a journal tracking your social patterns over a few weeks. Note what environments and types of interactions left you feeling satisfied or restless. Also, pay attention to your mood after isolation versus constant stimulation.

Gradually, these observations about your communication style, energy levels, and traits will help you recognize your natural social orientation. From there, you can play to your inherent strengths while developing lesser areas by stretching beyond your natural comfort zones.

EMBRACING YOUR UNIQUENESS

With self-awareness comes accepting your authentic social inclinations rather than forcing your identity to fit rigid expectations. Celebrate, not criticize, personality diversity. There are no "right" or "wrong" social temperaments; there are simply individual differences.

Once you discern your social orientation after honest self-appraisal, the next step involves fully embracing your uniqueness rather than fighting your innate predisposition. Introverts, remember that seeking occasional solitude to reenergize reflects a valid need, not awkward anti-sociality. Extroverts, feel free to express your social nature without restraint. Ambiverts, enjoy the freedom of interacting in any way you choose.

Beyond acceptance lies recognizing the comparative strengths of each personality type. While introverts may find small talk draining, they tend to excel at deep one-on-one conversations. Extroverts find ease in mixing among groups, enabling them to bridge fresh connections. The adaptability of ambiverts allows them to flow between roles. Each personality brings different strengths to the table.

Growth depends on nurturing your strengths while acknowledging areas for improvement rather than frustration at any perceived weaknesses. Introverts in leadership may require public speaking practice despite preferring behind-the-scenes roles. Extroverts may need teaching when their dominance overwhelms group discussions.

Most importantly, remember that social styles remain fluid across life stages. They are not fixed formulas. Embracing your present tendencies doesn't limit any future potential. Do your best to step outside your comfort zone and leverage your stronger skills.

NAVIGATING SOCIAL HIERARCHIES AND CLIQUES

The hallways of every high school comprise complex social ecosystems with unspoken codes that determine popularity and influence. While academics formally structure your days, intricate hierarchies silently dictate peer social structures and group dynamics after the bell rings.

In this section, we'll unravel the enigma of teen social stratification. We'll demystify the unwritten rules that guide peer conformity and inclusion within certain circles. We'll also help you determine your authentic affinities and then strategically join friend groups that uphold your values. With maturity comes recognizing that social labels hold fleeting importance compared to the character bonds that nurture personal growth.

We will also tackle the perpetual challenge of navigating peer pressure. You'll learn that by establishing boundaries and support systems beforehand, you can resist internalizing negative influences. We'll encourage you to uphold the courage of your convictions when you face social challenges rather than compromise your integrity to conform.

The Unspoken Rules of Teen Social Groups

Within teenage social spheres, intricate unwritten codes of conduct dictate behaviors, styles, and values that members must adopt to gain acceptance. Although often mystifying to navigate, decoding these subtle yet imperative group norms proves essential for teens hoping to ascend social ladders, avoid ridicule, or simply fit in.

To begin, take time to observe a social group's dynamics before attempting to join. Discern which students hold influence or perceived "cool" status. Notice what clothing brands earn kudos versus eye-rolls. Listen for slang terms and speaking patterns unique to the group. Understand that conforming to specific looks, lingo, and cultural references carries weight in wider membership appeals.

However, recognize that high school social hierarchies depend heavily on trends, contexts, and time. A group's popularity can rise and fall rapidly as students shift interests or rebel against the old guard. The "it crowd" stands on shaky ground. Remain open to fluid social currents as new leaders arise across ages and subcultures.

In today's digital era, online platforms heavily influence teenage social stratification as well. Instagram followers, Snapchat scores, or TikTok hearts quantify social cachet with hard numbers, whereas before, status remained vague or gossip-based. Because of this, creating an influential social media persona holds very real offline consequences for group status. But remember, this virtual caste system remains just as unpredictable.

The temptation will always exist to alter your personality and sacrifice your core values while striving to join the so-called "in crowd." But basing your self-worth on validation from exclusive social groups risks emotional distress when inevitable fallouts happen. Instead, look for friend circles and activities that align with your authentic passions and values first and foremost. As the tides shift, you will retain intrinsic self-assuredness regardless of external high school drama.

While evolving social codes will remain challenging to constantly track, their mystique diminishes significantly after you take a closer look. By proactively trying to understand groups before seeking to join them, you can gauge alignment and make informed social decisions rather than follow arbitrarily follow the crowd. Remember that what holds sway today passes tomorrow. Base your friendships and affiliations not on pressure to bend to the whims of the high school hierarchy but on the kindred spirits standing beside you during social changes.

Where Do You Fit In?

Influential social groups are different across high school subcultures —from athletes to artists to academic standouts. You must first identify friend circles that suit your individual interests and values rather than force uncomfortable attempts to join one exclusive clique.

Assess your core interests, causes, style sensibilities, and humor. Observe classmates who display shared passions or intellectual curiosity. Start conversations to see if your values align. Bond over beloved creative inspirations, whether you're an author, activist, or artist.

After identifying a promising social fit based on substance over mere surface popularity, put yourself outside your comfort zone by interacting with members. Have patience, as authentic relationships form slowly. Trust that bonds of friendship cement gradually through inside jokes and vulnerable conversations. Your common humanity will surface behind any initial social masks. Soon, a new group can feel like family, united by meaning underneath school survival.

While a chief friend group can help form your sense of belonging, it's also important to recognize the value of connections across diverse cliques to broaden your perspective. The principal clarinetist who is also passionate about meteorology merits friendship with both orchestra members and environmental club activists. Take time to discover these rich intersections that transcend traditional social boundaries.

Ultimately, the social niches you are in during adolescence don't matter as much as the kindred spirits you meet along the journey who feel like home. In navigating youth's messy quest to find yourself, you inevitably must try on and then shed several identities before self-clarity settles with maturity. Focus less on what preppy label fits and more on who helps you feel seen inside for who you are and hope to be.

Dealing With Peer Pressure

As you balance your need for independence with wanting peer approval, navigating peer pressure poses inevitable challenges that require a solid internal foundation. By establishing personal boundaries and clear value systems, you can resist unsafe conformity.

Before facing situations such as party invites or dares, reflect on what behaviors align with your values and what risks exceed your comfort levels. Knowing lines to not cross makes reacting quickly easier when pressure mounts suddenly. Open communication with trusted friends and mentors provides support to help weigh difficult decisions.

When faced with peers coaxing you to break rules or compromise your values, it is essential to feel confident in saying no. True friends will respect your autonomy and express disagreement compassionately. You can explain your reasons without judging the choices of others. You can suggest safer alternatives that show willpower and not killjoy tendencies.

Recognize that the influence of your peers often stems from your profound need for social bonds and fears of rejection or judgment by groups you admire. Building your self-esteem will allow you to rely less on the validation of others. Find groups that appreciate diversity and intellectual autonomy over conformity.

Uphold the courage of your personal convictions by drawing inspiration from positive role models who lead groups, not by domineering peer pressure but by unified visions—from youth activists to conscientious team captains. Internalizing their wisdom helps you make challenging judgment calls.

WRAPPING UP...

Understanding social dynamics in teen friend groups and cliques is hard but important. Just watching others does not reveal all the unspoken rules that make people popular. True understanding starts from within yourself.

By thinking about what you like socially and what matters to you, you can choose friend groups that fit your personality. Do not simply chase popularity with no meaning. Seek people who embrace the real you.

Also, know your strengths as a listener, organizer, or connector. Use those talents to help peers rather than change yourself to fit in. True leadership comes from uniting people around shared interests, not demanding followers.

Self-awareness also gives you the confidence to resist negative peer pressure. You can act from your values outward. As we next explore how personality shapes your communication style, remember self-knowledge is key to social success.

The social landscape always changes, but the one steady foundation for good relationships is you. Keep checking your inner compass so you can adjust your style but not lose your way with individuals or groups. Next, we dig deeper into personal patterns and flexibility. For now, keep learning through self-reflection. Your unique gifts are exactly what your widening social circles need—if you bravely share them. This light can then guide peers to find their own and bridge social divides. Our journey continues...

2

THE POWER OF SELF-AWARENESS

"The first step toward change is awareness. The second step is acceptance."

— NATHANIEL BRANDEN

This quote from Nathaniel Branden emphasizes the importance of self-awareness as the first step in personal growth and positive change, which is a valuable lesson as you and your peers navigate paths of self-discovery and development.

Do you know what emotions shape your decisions, actions, and reactions? Can you trace back a disagreement to the underlying trigger that caused you to flip your lid? Do you understand the strengths and growth opportunities that subtly influence your relationships?

Self-awareness means consciously understanding the inner drivers behind our outward expressions. It means bravely looking at our past experiences and learning from them so we can move forward from a place of understanding rather than continue to use default defenses. Self-awareness frees us from acting on autopilot and allows our inner values to guide our choices.

On the journey toward self-knowledge, we have to look below the surface and ask questions like:

- Where do my beliefs about myself and the world come from?
- How do distorted thought patterns impact my self-talk?
- What unresolved pain causes me to overreact?

Peeling back these layers opens the door to incredible self-realization and self-healing.

In this chapter, we'll hold up mirrors to see ourselves clearly so we can act and interact from a place of authenticity rather than fear or confusion. We'll sort out the puzzle pieces that comprise personality, wounds, hopes, and purpose. This self-excavation will fuel personal growth, propelling you to social excellence.

So, let's begin this fascinating adventure into the deepest parts of you! I promise that the destination of self-discovery will be well worth any uncomfortable moments the path may hold.

DISCOVERING THE INNER YOU

Understanding yourself on a deeper level is the key to unlocking social intelligence and creating more meaningful relationships. Self-awareness separates the conscious actor from the unwitting reactor. As the ancient Greek aphorism advises us: "Know thyself."

This journey of self-discovery will reveal your unique rhythms, tendencies, triggers, and gifts. It will shine light on the values, beliefs, and expectations that filter your perceptions and determine your choices. Understanding these layers will offer surprising insight and a feeling of freedom.

Social skills begin with self-skills. In this chapter, we'll peel the onion of your self, so to speak, and examine the central aspects that shape your internal experiences and outward expressions. What principles guide you? How do you make decisions? What knocks you off your center? Where do you shine? The work of questioning, listening, feeling, and adjusting never ends as life continues to mold you, but self-understanding gives you the power to steer your growth.

The unexamined life will always feel vaguely dissatisfying as you unconsciously play roles, follow the scripts of others, and lack a centered core. However, turning the lens inward makes life's puzzle pieces fit together. You step into the director role on the stage of your life. So, let the self-discoveries begin!

Your Values and Beliefs

Your values and beliefs shape how you see the world and interact with others. As a teen, you are still developing your personal value system based on your upbringing, life experiences, and evolving perspectives. It is important to take time for self-reflection to identify and assess your values and beliefs around key areas such as family, friends, school, activities, society, and culture.

What principles guide your thoughts and actions? What ideals are non-negotiable for you? What behaviors do you judge as right or wrong? Contemplating these questions reveals your values. Keep an open mind and avoid judging differing value systems while you gain clarity on what rings true for you.

When you have alignment between your values and actions, you build self-confidence and integrity. For example, if equality is a core value but you remain silent in the face of bullying, self-doubt may creep in. On the other hand, speaking up aligns with your values and feels empowering. This internal harmony brings peace.

In social settings, recognize that others may hold values that are different from yours. For instance, you may value adventurous experiences while your friend prefers predictability. Respecting differences demonstrates maturity and preserves relationships. However, with core values like honesty and respect, standing firm helps you maintain your self-respect.

As you evolve, some of your values may shift. Remain open to growth, but change from a place of truth rather than compromise. Recognize the times when flexibility strengthens your character versus compromising it. With values as your inner compass, it will become second nature to act authentically. You can handle any situation with grace and confidence.

Your Strengths and Weaknesses

Knowing your innate talents and skills that come naturally gives you social confidence and areas where you can contribute. It is equally important to be aware of your weaknesses, or those qualities that require your focused effort to develop. Honest self-assessment in both areas will reveal a path for growth.

You can assess personality tests and reflection questions to help reveal your aptitudes. However, direct feedback provides an objective lens for addressing any blind spots. Listen openly as loved ones highlight strengths you may take for granted and gently note areas where you could improve. Remember to receive feedback as a gift rather than a judgment.

Celebrate your signature strengths, as long as you remain open-minded, not arrogant. Similarly, approach your weaknesses from a growth mindset versus self-criticism. The only true failure is refusing to learn. Dedicate time to improve while operating from your strengths.

In social settings, rely on your strengths while minimizing your limitations. A charismatic public speaker can inspire a group's vision while a detailed planner can orchestrate the strategy. Knowing and playing to your strengths while supporting the abilities of others is how you create an effective team.

Your growth depends on putting in the work around your limitations. Set SMART goals (specific, measurable, attainable, relevant, and time-bound) to address your vulnerabilities and commit to a development plan. You can nurture new skills by returning to uncomfortable tasks until they become second nature. Involving trusted adults or friends can provide helpful accountability.

Above all, lovingly accept the whole you, perfections and imperfections alike. Work to build your confidence from real strengths while proactively improving your limitations. No matter what social situation you find yourself in, focus on continuous personal growth.

Your Emotional Triggers

In social settings, you may react strongly to seemingly innocent comments or behaviors without understanding why. These big responses are likely linked to an emotional trigger—something that hits a raw nerve and activates painful or powerful memories and feelings.

Triggers often come from negative experiences, especially from childhood. A teacher criticizing your work may subconsciously remind you of long-buried shame from a hyper-critical parent. An innocent teasing remark could bring up buried humiliation from past bullying. Your brain instinctively pulls from its memory bank to protect you, but the reaction can sometimes be problematic.

When you feel highly emotional, turn to proven coping strategies to self-soothe before you respond. A few helpful coping strategies include:

- naming the feelings that are surfacing and allowing them to pass through you
- breathing consciously while you picture a peaceful image
- seeking a timeout from the situation

These techniques short-circuit your brain's knee-jerk reaction, allowing logic to help regulate the intense feelings.

To heal the emotional bruise, you can have a thoughtful conversation with a trusted friend, adult, or mental health professional. Speak your truth about the origin of the hurt and release the negative charge of the trauma. If you're still struggling, forgiveness, grief work, or talk therapy can help alleviate triggering events from the past.

While triggers may always cause an initial pang, having self-awareness and regulation skills can significantly reduce their influence. Meditation and breathwork can strengthen the mind-body connection and bolster your resilience when someone or something pushes your buttons. Expect emotional flare-ups to occasionally ambush you, but stay centered in self-knowledge and they will not define or control you.

BUILDING A POSITIVE SELF-CONCEPT

While self-awareness shines a light on your inner self, self-concept shapes the attitudes you carry as you navigate the social landscape. Your fundamental beliefs about your abilities, attributes, and worthiness become a self-fulfilling prophecy, dictating what you attempt, what you expect, and what you allow.

In this critical section, we'll build the foundation for confidence and success by actively crafting an empowering self-concept. As we reframe self-perceptions, take ownership of our capabilities, and surround ourselves with positive reflections from others, we solidify the vision of our highest selves.

The seeds of self-belief you plant today shape the social destiny you grow into. Water them with bold aspirations rather than doubts. Nourish them by collecting evidence of your brilliance and belonging. Tend to them by filtering out negativity. Soon, these seeds will sprout robust certainties rather than fragile wishes. You will stand firmly rooted in self-knowledge, extending branches of courage and leaves of promise into any relationship or situation you encounter.

Self-Esteem and Social Confidence

Self-esteem refers to the overall opinion you hold of yourself, including your value and worthiness. This perception starts forming in childhood and evolves continuously based on your experiences and feedback from others. High self-esteem correlates strongly with social success, as you project and receive energy through this lens.

To build confidence before and during social interactions, focus on your strengths and the unique qualities you contribute. Do an affirmation exercise highlighting your talents, gifts, and positive intentions. Visualize being at ease, enjoying humor and curiosity. This will elevate positive emotions and transmit them to others.

While constructive confidence attracts people to you, destructive arrogance tends to repel. Remaining humble and strike a balance between self-assuredness and openness to learning. Consider that the brightest glow comes from light that is shared generously rather than a harsh glare. When you nurture your self-esteem, it uplifts you and those around you.

Often, fear of judgment prevents people from fully engaging and projecting their best selves. However, you must recognize that most people appreciate sincerity over perfection. You connect best when you are relaxed in your natural personality. Besides, other people's opinions of you reveal more about them—so value your own perception first.

Surround yourself with those who see, encourage, and champion the real you. Their warm acceptance will help dissolve any lingering negative self-perception you may have. In turn, you can become part of a positive peer support ecosystem, generously appreciating the light in others. This mutual understanding creates confidence.

When you reinforce self-esteem from within and without, you can step boldly into rewarding social connections.

Your Narrative

The stories we tell ourselves about our past, present, and future become the lens that shapes our social interactions. These inner narratives influence what we project, how we perceive others, and which opportunities we pursue. Just as a confident persona attracts, a negative storyline turns away.

Monitor your self-talk and correct negative distortions with balanced truths. Counteract messages like "I'm invisible" or "I'm too awkward" with empowering affirmations about your inherent strengths, talents, and positive qualities.

To improve your outlook, re-author the narratives around past social troubles. Rewrite scenes where you were excluded from the play as opportunities to discover a new creative passion. Frame painful rejections as nudges toward a better destiny. Infuse your history with new meaning.

As you present an authentic image, you will realize that everyone has parts of their story that are meant only for trusted ears. Sharing these stories is earned through exchanges of vulnerability. Look for cues that signal safety and receptivity. Answer sensitive questions with discretion to maintain appropriate boundaries and build close, trusted relationships.

As the main character in your epic life tale, wield the pen mightily but not carelessly. Tell empowering stories that illuminate your unique impact, including lessons you've learned and goals you've achieved. Write new promising chapters daily while making peace with past plot points. How your narrative unfolds depends profoundly on the self-talk in your head and heart.

Goal-Setting for Social Growth

To build social skills incrementally, apply the SMART goal framework when targeting areas for improvement. Define *specific* actions, *measurable* evidence of progress, and *achievable* and *relevant* behaviors practiced consistently within a defined *timeline*.

Rather than expect an overnight personality transformation, set modest goals like "giving five sincere compliments daily" or "making conversation with two new people per week." Small wins build your confidence to gradually expand your comfort zone.

When you are establishing broader life goals around academics, fitness, hobbies, or relationships, consider including a social skill component. For example, commit to asking teachers, coaches, and friends for performance feedback as part of your self-improvement vision.

Journal about challenges you've experienced when pursuing goals and make course corrections as needed. Review your patterns around successes as well. Discover your optimal rhythm, environment, and learning style for changes that require new neural pathways. And remember: Celebrate milestones enthusiastically.

True social skills stem from emotional intelligence combined with effective communication strategies. Setting intentional goals focused on shifting your mindset and behaviors builds a critical foundation. Soon, making and deepening connections will become organic rather than mechanical. Applaud each evidence of emerging grace, warmth, and social intuition. The results will speak for themselves.

MINDFULNESS AND SELF-REFLECTION

Beyond conscious awareness, social skills also depend on present-moment awareness during interactions. Mindfulness practices can train your ability to tune into emotional undercurrents within and between people. This attention creates empathy and harmony. Likewise, reflecting on encounters for patterns over time accelerates your self-understanding.

Mindfulness and self-reflection foster clarity on your rhythms, triggers, talents, and blind spots. It helps you notice what energizes you socially and what drains you emotionally. These lenses become crucial as you intentionally build a rich network or seek deeper friendships.

In this section, we'll cover core mindfulness techniques that will allow you to stay grounded when conversations get complicated. You'll also establish a journaling practice to externalize key lessons and realizations from social exchanges. Regular reflection like this will help you accelerate your skill-building.

Additionally, you'll learn the art of receiving feedback. Truly hearing how others perceive you, though sometimes uncomfortable, can highlight areas for growth that you cannot provide alone. Incorporating this outside input with your internal discoveries can create unparalleled social agility.

By repeatedly looking inward through various angles while interacting outwardly with presence and care, your social intelligence will reach new depths. You will become a true master of building and maintaining relationships.

The Role of Mindfulness in Social Interaction

Mindfulness means purposefully bringing non-judgmental awareness to the present moment versus dwelling on regrets or hypotheticals. Tuning into your thoughts, emotions, and senses without analysis creates clarity. Studies confirm that practicing mindfulness reduces stress, increases emotional intelligence, and enhances relationships (Jiménez-Picón et al., 2021).

Being fully present and attentive in social situations shows respect and care for others. Before entering a gathering, pause to arrive consciously rather than rushing in mentally scattered. Set an intention to move slowly, listen deeply, and meet eyes warmly. These behaviors reflect the inner calm that mindfulness cultivates.

When conversations trigger uncomfortable emotions, ground yourself with subtle mindful techniques. Focus on your feet connecting with the floor, the sensation of clothing on your skin, or the process of inhaling and exhaling. This can reset an agitated nervous system so you can then return to the conversation feeling centered and thoughtful.

Seeking first to understand rather than be understood requires mindfulness. This means allowing others to express themselves fully before you respond. Notice how a person's body language can communicate as much as their words. Reflect on your perceptions to make sure that you understand what's being said. This art of empathetic listening helps strengthen relationships.

Even if you have only a few minutes each day, try to incorporate mindfulness practices into your daily habits. Try meditating, keeping a gratitude journal, taking technology-free nature walks, or doing an artistic hobby. As you go throughout your day, notice the beauty and meaning around you. This helps infuse your interactions with warmth and presence.

The Art of Self-Reflection

Self-improvement depends profoundly on self-reflection, which is the habit of examining your social experiences to find insights for better relationships and outcomes. Journaling after interactions is an excellent way to create space for contemplation. Over time, you'll see clear patterns emerge to inform wiser actions.

Schedule regular journaling periods to download your thoughts and feelings about social exchanges, especially those that create intense emotions. Free writing can help you find clarity. Recording details cements learning and helps you notice patterns over time. Digital journals also conveniently timestamp your entries.

Beyond simply chronicling events, question your assumptions, reactions, and role in various situations. Ask thoughtful questions like:

- What false narratives do I have?
- How did my triggers or biases influence my interactions?
- What lessons can I learn for the future?

This reflection bears the fruits of growth.

Celebrate discoveries about the communication style, conflict resolution approach, and rapport-building techniques that work well for you. Identify areas that need improvement without self-judgment. Everyone has social strengths and struggles while navigating this learning curve.

True self-knowledge comes from questioning, listening, adjusting, and maturing through life's classroom. Regular reflection serves as a compass guiding your developmental path. However, beware of analysis paralysis! Balance thinking and journaling with concrete actions that apply the lessons you've learned day by day.

Feedback and Growth

While self-examination offers one mirror, trusted advisors provide an exterior reflection that can reveal blind spots. Regularly ask close friends, family members, and mentors how they experience you in relationships. Listen without defensiveness to pinpoint areas for social and emotional growth.

To benefit from feedback, first understand the intent behind suggestions. Supportive critiques aim to empower you while toxic attacks can undermine your confidence. Consider the source of the feedback and their experience mentoring growth in others.

Once you know that the motivation is constructive, apply the insights as a tool for self-improvement, not as a weapon against yourself. Avoid excessive self-criticism by balancing reflection on limitations with celebration of strengths. Use this feedback to create practical goals for continued progress.

Everyone misses social cues sometimes or acts unconsciously. Remembering that we are all human can help defuse any shame triggered by critiques. Self-compassion helps you digest difficult experiences and integrate lessons with humility, patience, and care.

The twin foundations of deep self-knowledge and receptivity to the perspectives of others strengthen the emotional muscles you need for rewarding relationships. Regularly scheduling feedback conversations with compassionate guides reinforces your resilience by facing your flaws, sharpening your social skills, and optimizing your behaviors. Soon, you will be able to handle any interaction with increased wisdom.

CASE STUDY: JADA

When 16-year-old Jada was passed over for the lead role in the school musical that she had confidently expected to land, she fell into a state of confusion and despair, wondering "What's wrong with me?" Her outspoken mother, Amari, went straight to the drama teacher, Mrs. Fields, to argue that Jada deserved

the lead and ask what weaknesses led to this poor decision.

Embarrassed by her mother's aggressive reaction, Jada asked friends if she seemed arrogant about her abilities. They reassured Jada of her talent but noted how she could sometimes dominate conversations rather than listen to input from others. Jada reflected on past auditions and recalled focusing intensely on her own performance rather than interacting with scene partners.

This feedback prompted Jada's self-discovery about the underlying insecurities driving her. She realized that always feeling like the "oddball artsy kid" fed an obsessive need to prove herself creatively, and this manifested through overbearing behavior. With these hard truths revealed through self-reflection, Jada felt ready to transform.

Jada asked both her mother and Mrs. Fields for a conversation to humbly apologize and share breakthroughs about understanding the unhealthy motivations behind her conduct. Releasing defenses opened a dialogue for mutual sharing about past hurts and future hopes. Reconstruction began through self-awareness leading to accountability, forgiveness, maturity, and reconciliation.

WRAPPING UP...

With greater clarity about your inner landscape through self-awareness practices, you can now cross the bridge from self-knowledge to skillful interaction by exploring the art of communication. How you convey or receive information impacts the quality of any relationship.

Self-awareness builds the foundation of authenticity, emotional intelligence, and inner security to show up fully present with others. Communication skills determine how gracefully you relate once engaged socially. Do your words uplift and inspire? Do you listen with care and discernment?

In the next chapter, we'll build proficiency across the verbal and nonverbal aspects of communication. We will learn to initiate conversations, cultivate dialogue with presence, read cues in body language, resolve breakdowns, and tailor messaging for digital mediums.

Just as self-awareness separates conscious actors from unwitting reactors, tools of effective communication distinguish great connectors from those left confused by relational complexities. Let's now embark on elevating your expression and interpretation abilities to masterfully dance through all of life's relationships.

3
COMMUNICATION ESSENTIALS

"The single biggest problem in communication is the illusion that it has taken place."

— GEORGE BERNARD SHAW

This insight from legendary playwright George Bernard Shaw points to the pitfalls tripping up even the most sincere

attempts to connect. We often assume that what we said was received as intended. We suppose that our listening showed true understanding. We expect words of affirmation to heal without being distorted.

How sadly but commonly this proves untrue! In real life, signals get crossed, filters discolor our original meaning, and assumptions create unintended consequences. Soon enough, two parties leave the conversation thinking all is well, but they have actually failed to communicate!

In this chapter, we'll unpack the essential elements for giving and receiving messages that communicate clearly across the intricate bridges between our hearts and minds. We'll learn both elegant self-expression and artful inquiry to captivate audiences. We'll practice listening beyond merely hearing words and move to comprehend the meaning and spirit behind what people are saying. We'll work to be attuned to the nonverbal dimensions of body language that qualify and amplify verbal content.

Master communicators recognize consciousness as an intricate tapestry that is continually spoken and respoken into being. They weave their words mindfully, discerning vital threads that compose interpersonal harmony versus those that unknowingly unravel the fabric of communication. Our relationships thrive or suffer based on these choices. Let's look at the tools that can elevate your social intelligence to this higher level, beginning with decoding the mysteries of messaging, listening, understanding, and connecting.

MASTERING VERBAL COMMUNICATION

Words carry creative power. How we articulate experiences and ideas impacts our relationships, determines our understanding, and seeds our future possibilities. Likewise, carefully hearing others recognizes human dignity.

In this foundational section, we'll build verbal communication skills to set you apart as an influential connector, compassionate confidant, and magnetic leader. We'll balance graceful self-expression with artful inquiry. We'll mindfully listen not just to reply but to truly understand.

You will learn to start enriching conversations that tap into inspiration rather than canned responses. Your questions will mine wisdom and summon untold truths. Soon, your authentic presence will grace social gatherings with meaning.

Speaking with insight, listening with care, and keeping space for silence differentiate communication that simply informs from dialogue that transforms. Here, we'll elevate your verbal mastery to this higher level. The world awaits the gifts your voice will unlock!

The Art of Conversation

Conversations create connections when people feel seen and heard. Speaking purposefully, listening attentively, building responsively, and respecting pacing allow you to communicate with trust and depth. When you master give-and-take dynamics, it builds rewarding relationships.

Rather than dread small talk, view conversations as adventures in discovering common ground and new perspectives. Allow natural curiosity about a person's essence or experiences to guide your questions. Match their enthusiasm and tone instead of interrogating them.

Be aware of talking time compared to listening. Quieting your inner monologue lets others' words reach your brain. Reframe "listening to respond" to "listening to understand." Resist interrupting even if you risk forgetting an idea. If needed, capture your thoughts in a notebook to reflect on later.

Mindfully choose words that fit the nature of the relationship. Concrete language clarifies what you mean while metaphorical speech can inspire. Your tone conveys as much meaning as the words you use. Inflect appropriately to align your expressions with your intentions. Avoid sarcasm or ambiguity, which can create misunderstandings.

Remembering names and asking informed follow-up questions shows that you care for an individual's uniqueness. Repeat their name in the introduction and in your mind when you respond. Reference earlier dialog details to reinforce recall, focus, and authentic interest. You honor others by remembering what matters to them.

Active Listening Skills

Unlike passive hearing, when you actively listen, you intentionally concentrate to understand what a person is saying and feeling. Part of active listening is facing the speaker, establishing eye contact, and mirroring their body language to demonstrate engaged attention that fosters trust and depth.

When you're listening, avoid distractions and multitasking, which signal that you're mentally checked out. Quiet any inner dialogue that is judging a person's tone or crafting a response. Instead, focus solely on absorbing their words, intentions, and emotions. Nod understandingly while allowing pauses for their reflections.

Mindfully notice nonverbal cues that go along with verbal content. Facial expressions can show anxiety despite a calm tone; light-hearted laughter can reveal deeper dynamics for an authentic response.

Common listening pitfalls include rehearsing replies rather than truly responding, interrupting someone with your perspectives, or redirecting the conversation to yourself. Catch when your attention drifts and redirect it gently back to the speaker.

You can improve your active listening skills through ongoing practice. Allow others to summarize without interruption to check on your ability to be receptive. Ask clarifying questions about anything you don't understand or want to know more about. Soon, your focused presence will uplift your communication.

Asking Engaging Questions

Questions invite others to reveal more about themselves and their experiences. Well-crafted questions demonstrate how much you care about peoples' stories. However, the quality of your questions determines whether conversations stagnate politely or thrive authentically.

Open-ended questions like "What made you so passionate about this?" unlock deeper sharing. These types of questions pull for anecdotal responses rather than single-word answers and enrich connections. Once you're comfortable, you can ask increasingly transparent questions to reveal motivations and meaning.

Save closed-ended questions that gather only straightforward information for early interactions. Asking deep questions too quickly without context can make people instinctively guard their more sensitive thoughts. Be attentive and patient as you ask more meaningful questions.

Encourage people to elaborate through gentle nudges like "Tell me more" or connective comments like "That happened to me once too!" This encourages sharing within a safe space. Offer empathy and non-judgment regardless of what emerges.

While your inquisitiveness oils social gears, invasive prying can corrode trust. Read signs like hesitation in overstepping lines. Questions should open doors, not flood private spaces. Master this nuance to help maintain mutual trust.

NONVERBAL COMMUNICATION CUES

Beyond verbal content, communication equally unfolds through subtle body language that conveys what words cannot. The angle of someone's shoulders can hint at confidence or withdrawal. A person's hand gestures can punctuate unsaid meaning. The warmth in a friend's eyes can bond souls faster than any carefully crafted phrase. We transmit paragraphs through invisible signals that can manifest as goosebumps, blushing, and breath changes picked up by intuitive communicators.

This silent sensory transmission can mold impressions profoundly. Without conscious awareness, we undermine bold claims through slumped posture and betray twinges of anxiety in furrowed brows. We unconsciously leak mistrust or regard through micro-expressions. We cannot hide what our body broadcasts.

In this section, you'll develop literacy in reading these physical messages that qualify spoken language with feeling, intention, and history. You learn to align your outward expression with your inner truth by better occupying your energy. You'll match movements to moods and boundaried touch for support rather than confusion. Soon, your body language will align with your messaging to magnify rather than distort relationships through mixed signals.

Expect connections to deepen rapidly as your social radar fine-tunes!

The Silent Language of Body Language

While words speak, body language can shout volumes. Your posture can convey confidence or nerves, crossed arms can show defense, and leaning in can communicate interest. Pay attention to these nonverbal messages. Here are a few ways to get started:

- Study body language in videos and photos to understand common patterns and meanings. Practice your body language using a mirror or videos.
- Consciously shift your stance to control what you're saying rather than unconsciously send mixed signals.
- Mimic the posture of others to build quick rapport in early interactions.
- Take pauses to notice hand gestures. Restless feet can mean impatience. Smiling eyes can mean relaxation.
- Evaluate how your nonverbal language aligns or contradicts the words you're speaking.
- Make small gestures more intentionally dramatic to reinforce verbal messaging.
- Lean forward with furrowed brows for serious topics or stand loosely waving arms when describing lighthearted memories.

Recognize that generational and cultural backgrounds can influence comfort with touch, personal space, and direct eye contact. Customize nonverbals to respect the norms of those engaged while affirming boundaries. Research common nonverbal communication conventions in cultures you interact with frequently. Adjust your proximity, touch, and eye contact accordingly to avoid miscommunications. Over time, cross-cultural body language literacy improves relationships and minimizes discomfort on either side.

Ongoing mindfulness creates optimal responses. Whenever tensions heighten, interrupt by centering your breath and equilibrium. Soon, these second-nature mannerisms will help foster rapport subliminally with a diverse social spectrum. In triggered moments, press your palms together firmly or stretch your arms wide to regain composure subtly before responding. Use quick meditative tactics between interactions to reset any lingering frustration or anxiety from previous conversations.

The Power of Eye Contact

Our eyes channel tremendous sensitivity and power (deGrasse Tyson, 2001). Gazing into someone's eyes can feel profoundly intimate. Limited eye contact can be perceived as nonchalance and may signal dismissal rather than shyness. Monitor this dynamic carefully. Practice varying eye contact duration with friends to expand your comfort zone. Imagine sending compassion or reassurance directly from your heart through your eyes to deepen connections nonverbally.

Unbroken eye contact can equally intimidate when it is prolonged past comfort. Experiment with reading reactions to various eye contact intervals. Regularly meet the eyes of shy speakers then look away warmly. This builds connections without overpowering others. Avoid staring contests unless you intend to establish dominance. If others show anxiety or glance away frequently, offer a gentle smile and tilt your head to accept rather than demand attention.

While direct eye contact reads confidently, indirect glances also reassure. Balance comfort for yourself and your counterparts based on your intention. Let settings guide what is appropriate. Regardless, maintain friendly visual engagement throughout your interactions. Briefly look down when you're thinking to relieve intensity, but keep flickering eye contact to sustain engagement. When you're on the phone, envision making eye contact to help you connect with the person on the other end.

The Subtleties of Space and Touch

Those who have mastered social skills understand how to respect personal space. To improve your skills:

- Note how others lean in or away as a conversation unfolds.
- Give breathing room unless the other person's gestures welcome closeness.
- Reserve touch only for those you trust deeply.
- Step slightly closer to gauge receptiveness before you assume another person's comfort level.
- Mirror the other person's movement.
- Catch yourself overstepping spatial boundaries and smoothly widen space, apologizing if necessary.

When conversing, move simultaneously if the other person shifts closer. If they seem uncomfortable, politely increase the distance. Learn cultural norms around appropriate contact to avoid missteps. You can lightly squeeze your friend's shoulder, pat their back, or graze their arm briefly when words fail to capture emotional gravity. However, limit outward touch to hands, arms, and shoulders rather than facial or any other regions suggestive of respect.

Soon, reading comfort zones will become automatic. You'll occupy any social situation smoothly through your sharp yet sensitive social radar. Even complicated nonverbal dynamics won't trip up the graceful style you're cultivating. As your sensory awareness grows, you can tune in to subtle cues that reveal deeper moods and adjust your message accordingly. Whether through eye warmth, close presence, or well-timed touch, your emotional support will be felt without saying a word.

DIGITAL CHATS: KEEPING IT CLEAR AND KIND

Beyond in-person and phone interactions, social connection increasingly unfolds online through written digital messages that can bridge any distance. Teens rely on texting, social media, and discussion forums for community support, identity exploration, and entertainment.

While virtual communication offers convenience through quick connections across distances, relying predominantly on digital messages rather than face-to-face interaction risks distortion or misinterpretation without tonal cues or body language to help you understand the intended meaning. Relationships can suffer without seeing tender smiles, hearing gentle reassurances, or touching hands for empathy. Personality nuance can also fade digitally. Yet, when handled thoughtfully, online spaces can help you create deep bonds that are unconstrained by social anxieties that can be present in face-to-face interactions.

In this section, we'll offer the best etiquette practices to uphold respect in messaging, emailing, and posting online. You'll learn to convey and interpret emoji-filled exchanges and prevent misunderstanding or unnecessary conflict. You'll represent your highest self through thoughtful profiles and comments that contribute to progressive social change rather than petty drama. Ultimately, you'll harness the incredible connectivity of technology while avoiding common pitfalls that can sabotage integrity or relationships when you rely too carelessly on digital interaction that lacks human dimensions.

Texting and Messaging

Digital chats allow you to connect quickly but can get confusing without hearing a tone or seeing someone's face. Follow "net manners" to avoid drama. Don't type in ALL CAPS or overuse !!! marks that might seem angry. Save those for special emphasis. Use emojis to liven things up, but focus more on kind words. Express care through questions and replies showing you are tuned in. Create inside jokes and make plans to meet up. Texting helps create stronger bonds when handled wisely.

Reply fairly fast when you can to show you care. However, you can also say if you'll be away from the phone for a bit so people don't wonder why you didn't text back. Schedule tech-free time to give your mind a break. Have fun with digital chats while remaining respectful. Allow others the freedom to respond on their own time while staying reasonably connected. Don't assume texts left on "read" mean passive rejection—offer people the benefit of the doubt. Extend patience and speak up supportively if feelings get hurt. Treat text relationships with the same care you would all relationships.

Emailing

When sending an email, craft clear subject lines so people see what it's about. Keep messages short and to the point after friendly hellos. Use proper grammar and words since emails spread easily out of context. Always double-check addresses before you press send! Express genuine care through warm sign-offs wishing people well. Send thoughtful thank yous when appropriate gestures are remembered. Follow up on requests showing completion and responsibility. Let organization and effort show in inboxes.

Show extra thought in emails even with friends. Express real thank yous for replies and give updates so friends know you appreciate them. Check in with people if you don't hear back, too. Building relationships takes effort, but it pays off! Send words of affirmation to lift friends when they need encouragement. Share good news and jokes to create positive associations. Bond over common frustrations with reasonable venting. Develop trust and depth in communicating beyond surface niceties.

Using Social Media

Be sure your posts match who colleges or employers would see. Show your talents and care while keeping personal stuff private. Share just enough to be relatable but not overexposed. Consider social platforms extended resumes that showcase your best qualities. Research your target schools and companies to guide appropriate content themes that could benefit your chances of getting accepted. Curate different profiles custom fit to purposes that serve rather than restrict your options.

Address tensions peacefully and seek first to understand differences. Words reach far on social media, so avoid careless remarks—even by accident. Admitting mistakes responsibly earns respect. Handle challenges smartly and your character shines through! Promote causes and organizations working for positive change to offset negative news feeds. Tag friends to appreciate their talents and accomplishments. Jump into supportive action during global or community crises to model your leadership initiative.

Post to connect authentically with care, wisdom, and kindness. Curate your profiles like an evolving book since posts stick around. Use your influence as a force for good. Share words, images, and media that inspire, inform, and uplift. Submit thoughtful comments on forums and repost quality content that benefits others. Your contributions compose an admirable autobiography of your life.

CASE STUDY: DEV

When 10th grader Dev noticed his friend Uma had seemed down lately, he felt determined to help lift her spirits. "You look a little off... Wanna talk so I can try to cheer you up with some dumb jokes?!" he asked casually, assuming she would appreciate his lighthearted caring gestures.

However, Uma snapped back defensively, "I said I'm FINE! Just leave me alone!" Dev felt blindsided and stung by her biting reaction, having meant well with his offer to listen. He avoided Uma for days before a mutual friend revealed she was struggling at home and felt isolated.

Dev realized he never created a safe space for Uma to confide her problems. By jumping straight to humorous banter, he missed the hints that she needed to process her pain first before joking. It hit Dev how easily miscommunication poisons connections despite best intentions. He humbly asked Uma if they could start fresh, and she nodded, wiping away tears while expressing appreciation for his effort to truly understand. They talked for hours, building new friendship depths neither expected.

WRAPPING UP...

When it comes to the fundamentals of verbal and nonverbal communication, we recognize that even with good intentions, misunderstandings and conflicts inevitably arise and can jeopardize relationships. Emotions flare defensively as criticisms feel personal or careless words spread surprisingly far out of context. Connection suffers without conflict literacy to navigate these messy nuances.

The communication journey requires building clarity skills and troubleshooting tools to restore understanding once there is a breakdown. We must address tensions courageously before there is lasting damage and remember to honor each person's unique perspective. This prevents natural disagreements from spiraling into resentment. After all, no one enjoys perpetual conflict, and each person shares responsibility for solutions.

Now that we have covered the foundational piece of harmonious interaction, we'll tackle the inevitable snags that can trip up even the most practiced communicators. You'll learn proven techniques for de-escalation, emotional self-regulation, boundary setting, and conflict mediation that apply beyond your teenage years into the professional realm. Let's take a look at the secrets master communicators use when stakes seem high and emotions run hot!

4

MAKING FRIENDS AND
BUILDING NETWORKS

"To succeed in life, you need two things: ignorance and confidence."

— MARK TWAIN

The world can feel increasingly disjointed, which makes the art of connecting meaningfully vital to your well-being. This chapter shows how you can create strong bonds, both online and off, that will help you weather life's storms. First, we'll look at timeless wisdom about how to cultivate profound friendship  through understanding beyond surface judgments. Then, we'll provide practical advice to help you expand your social networks through clubs, events, and savvy online engagement. Finally, we'll look at the principles of safety in navigating complex digital landscapes, which will allow you to foster connection without forfeiting your privacy or voice.

Technology is always evolving, but our core human needs remain the same. In this section, we'll look at how to protect that fragile heartbeat that binds us beneath the noise. We'll learn how to approach online spaces and new contacts with empathy first, considering our mutual desire for purpose and community. When divergent souls feel truly accepted as they are, our defensive walls begin to crumble and reveal the best in one another.

This progress requires compassion and conversations that gently uplift all parties. Where isolation can make us feel like we're in the dark, creating friendships and building networks can illuminate our lives. So, let's learn how to reach out. Powerful forces wait on the other side.

THE ART OF FRIENDSHIP

Meaningful human connection forms the fabric of a well-lived life. Beyond superficial relationships that may be rooted in utility, a profound bond with another person allows our best selves to emerge. The art of cultivating deep friendship reveals truths about human nature: that we thrive by being understood and that we want to know and be known without pretense. This section maps out friendship across its lifespan, looks at how rapport ignites through discovering shared outlooks, and shows how casual camaraderie can strengthen into vulnerable self-revelation between trusted friends over time. There may be obstacles that require patience when busy schedules limit your availability, and there may be times when you feel that you are giving more than you are receiving. However, resilient friendships adapt like oaks in storms—flexible, forgiving, and impervious to distance or time when two different personalities come together to offer unconditional support. These quiet miracles can weave lifelong connections, but friendships require care and feeding to grow strong. The good news is that the effort can yield meaningful bonds that will enrich your life.

Starting Friendships

When seeking new friendships, focus on finding shared passions, values, and experiences to establish rapport rather than trying to impress. Listen for subtle clues that suggest you have common outlooks that you can explore. Real connection centers on understanding, not showing off. Be genuine and let relationships unfold organically. While first impressions invite judgments, recognize that people and relationships evolve. Avoid pigeonholing new people prematurely. With time, you could discover unexpected depth. Reserve judgment until you truly know someone. Initiate contact gently, not aggressively, through warm curiosity rather than interrogation. It's normal to have some silence, so be patient. Try to create an open environment for sharing thoughts and feelings.

When you remember personal details, it shows that you care. You can even make discreet notes after conversations for follow-up later. These simple gestures acknowledge the other person's needs and can build lifelong bonds. This type of thoughtfulness fosters emotional connection. Learn to view your social bravery as an achievement, whatever the outcome. Each courageous conversation will expand your confidence for future interactions. Anxiety will eventually give way to hard-won social agility through these small daily risks, and your social skills will develop through practice and perseverance.

Deepening Bonds

Having casual friends may meet your surface needs, but close friends will help you wrestle with life's deep questions, spurring growth together. One type of friendship offers some comfort, and the other strengthens over time into a trusting bond through consistent nurturing. Invest in the relationships that fill your soul. Before you expect others to open up to you, generously listen and share about yourself. Maintain your healthy boundaries to prevent premature affection from jeopardizing budding connections. Close bonds require patient nurturing, not force. Go at the pace your friend sets and one that is also comfortable for you.

Nurture your connections with consistent emotional, mental, and practical support. Take turns making commitments. Pay kindness forward. This mutual care and investment fosters the strongest bonds. Give without expectation of return. However, assess if you receive as much as you give. If there is an imbalance, you can compassionately address the issue. Seek supportive friends who are your equals—you deserve reciprocal relationships.

It's okay to reconsider one-sided relationships. While casual friends have a purpose, reserve space and time for those who uplift you as much as you uplift them. Surround yourself with people who bring out your best self.

Sustaining Connections

Consistent care, not grand gestures, determines a friendship's lifespan. Frequent check-ins matter more than sporadic shows of support. However, you can always resume neglected connections when possible. It's never too late to revive a relationship. As a teenager, your priorities are evolving. You can embrace busier lives by adapting your communication to address shifting needs and interests. To maintain connections, try to accommodate changing circumstances compassionately.

Bonds can change gradually because of unexpected life changes. With forgiveness and patience, these transitions don't have to sever connections you have built on trust. Give your friends grace when they take diverging paths. People often grow in unpredictable ways. Using your communication skills can bridge this distance. Schedule check-ins to get updates from your friends. If you once had a good rapport, this simple contact can restore it. Being separated geographically doesn't mean you have to be separated emotionally.

When occasionally together with a friend, celebrate your personal growth since the last time you saw each other. Talk about good times in the past together. Some bonds don't need constant contact to maintain their meaning. When you were once close to someone, time and distance alone cannot dismantle that. Cherish these connections that endure despite how your lives are changing.

BUILDING YOUR SOCIAL NETWORK

Weaving bonds of support sustains the soul, yet many teens mourn shrinking social connections amid increasingly disjointed worlds. Though screens now mediate much of how we interface, our ancient need for belonging remains. This section will illuminate the pathways for you to enrich your community by broadening beyond your habitual bubbles. You'll discover vital networking principles for teens and adults, both online and off. You'll learn to successfully navigate digital and in-person gatherings. Traditional wisdom counsels us to move beyond divisions toward our shared humanity. When people feel truly heard and known, alienation makes way for friendship. First, you must build authentic bridges to your inner truths before welcoming others. Soon, where you once wandered lost, you'll find a community awaiting you.

Why Social Networks Matter

Having a wide social network has many benefits. It gives you access to more perspectives, resources, and opportunities. You also gain emotional support during hard times. Maintaining relationships takes effort but pays off exponentially. The more diverse contacts you have, the more knowledge and support will be available when challenges arise. Invest the time to widen your circle continuously.

Research shows that people with broader social connections are happier and healthier (Umberson & Karas Montez, 2011). They exhibit lower levels of anxiety and depression. Humans crave community and thrive when those needs are met. So, make social outreach a priority.

Connect With Different Groups

Get to know all kinds of people, those with similar and different backgrounds. After all, variety brings more learning. Look for shared interests to bond over. Seek common ground while respecting the contrasting views of others. Broadening your connections removes assumptions about entire groups. Find the humanity in each individual you interact with.

Prejudice stems largely from a lack of exposure to particular groups. Stretch your comfort zone by engaging respectfully with people of different ages, cultures, occupations, and viewpoints. Work hard to suspend your initial judgments; complexity lives beneath surfaces.

Strategies to Expand Your Network

Join clubs or volunteer groups to meet new people. Talk to friends of friends to widen your circle. Use social media sites to connect and then interact personally. As you get older, attend professional association meetings to make career contacts. Follow up with these connections quickly before you lose momentum. You could even set a goal for new contacts to make each month.

When conversing, shift the focus from touting your accomplishments to discovering the unfolding dreams of others. Ask insightful questions, then intently listen instead of passively waiting your next turn to speak. This type of curiosity and engagement attracts kindred spirits.

Leveraging Social Media

Platforms like Facebook help you nurture existing ties. Later, LinkedIn can facilitate professional networking. The key is transitioning online connections into real-life friendships. Comment, react, and share posts to deepen growing connections. Then, invite new online contacts to chat. Use video calls to maintain contact with friends all over the world.

Avoid over-reliance on social media alone to build your community; it is a helpful tool, but it can risk creating only superficial bonds. Cyber-messaging is meant to complement face-to-face, phone, and snail mail interactions woven into a whole-person connection. Use social media to create a multifaceted approach to communication.

"Six Degrees" in Reality

The idea behind "six degrees of separation" is that you are only six introductions away from anyone on Earth. So, don't hesitate to ask friends for connections! Networking multiplies your links exponentially. These degrees of separation disappear quickly when each person connects you with their contacts. Remember that each individual represents access to their own intricate web of relationships. Keep networking persistently to expand your reach.

When seeking particular resources, especially as you get older, don't hesitate to request referrals within your networks. While specific needs may not emerge immediately, plant seeds for future nurturing. You could even follow up with people you meet using handwritten notes to cement memorable impressions.

Networking Skills for Teens

Networking is about forming genuine connections, not just advancing yourself. Focus on listening, understanding perspectives, and discovering shared interests. Be curious about other people. Approach networking as a two-way street—emphasize giving rather than getting. Share your authentic self, and in return, learn from the diverse individuals you meet. This mutual understanding builds the strongest networks. Listen earnestly to understand, not just reply. Find common visions to unite around.

Mind Your Manners

Approach new contacts respectfully and professionally. Practice a confident handshake or introduction. Ask thoughtful questions to find common ground for bonding. Show integrity when facing hard choices. Your reputation travels quickly. Always lead with positivity online and off. Cyberbullying brews toxic reputations that can be hard to shake. Promote people and ideas rather than tearing them down. Uplift the dignity in everyone. This type of civility brings out the best in us.

Join In

Participate in clubs, volunteer projects, and part-time jobs to expand your network organically. Contribute value through your skills or enthusiasm. Discuss your ambitions to find possible mentors within these circles. Seek leadership roles in organizations that are aligned with your vision. As you gain more experience, manage committees and projects with maturity. Demonstrating that you are responsible builds your credibility. Don't be afraid to apply to competitive programs that will allow you to rub shoulders with elite peers.

Craft Your Story

As you prepare to enter higher learning or professional spaces, create a one-minute "elevator pitch" summarizing your passions, strengths, and goals. Tailor your message depending on the situation and listener while staying authentic. Refine your pitch through practice rounds with friends. Think of it as your personal commercial and come up with bullets that highlight your service activities, athletic and artistic pursuits, academic interests, and career ambitions. Memorize the details through repetition and polish them without over-scripting your delivery.

Find Mentors

Connect respectfully with accomplished professionals who are willing to advise you. Do your research to identify promising mentors who are aligned with your passions. Seek targeted counsel, but avoid over-relying on informal mentors. Check that the relationship is helpful for both of you. If you can't find initially someone, try to access leaders through cold contact and reference shared experiences from their career history. Flatter their accomplishments. Then, explain how their guidance could keep you from pitfalls they already navigated.

The Takeaway

Widen your network of positive connections through genuine interest in your community. Uplift others and ask for support when needed. Build your communication skills by balancing confidence with humility. Move forward with an open heart and focused vision. Stay true to your highest values and instincts. Redirect conversations subtly when you feel uneasy. Your future holds bright promise —each interaction moves you toward fulfilling your potential. Have faith in the inner wisdom guiding you.

Navigating Social Events

Approach new events with an open, positive attitude. Focus outward, not inward. Brief small talk helps adjust to the energy before you can start a meaningful conversation. Scan the room to identify familiar faces to help you settle in. Slow your speech and breathing to reduce anxiety. If you are still nervous remember that this too shall pass.

Circulate with purpose. Observe anyone standing alone, then warmly introduce yourself. Take an interest in their story. If a circle forms, listen first to gauge entry points before contributing your part. Chat briefly with wallflowers to make them feel included. Laugh generously to uplift spirits all around. A little levity energizes the room.

Look for nonverbal cues like eye contact welcoming you into ongoing conversations. Ask curious rather than closed-ended questions: "What most inspired your work?" rather than "Where do you work?" Actively listen for threads in the conversation that can weave together divergent perspectives. Try to find common ground in shared values rather than surface-level facts. It's okay if there is some silence while you wait for others to express their viewpoints.

Wrap Up Gracefully

When you're ready to move on, summarize the key points you found meaningful from the conversation before leaving on a high note. End with open-ended remarks that will allow future follow-up. Shake hands firmly and maintain direct eye contact to convey a memorable impact. You can also promise politely to continue the dialogue later. Try to exit organically when the energy wanes rather than leaving abruptly.

Jot down names and details discreetly if you think you'll forget. Then, you can reference conversations from the first meeting during the next interaction. If you told someone you would get back to them, send the requested information within 48 hours. The follow-through will solidify the positive impression you made. Handwrite personal notes referencing the specifics you discussed rather than generic form letters. Keep a list of contacts under niche tags so you can find them easily later. You can also add new acquaintances to your social media circles.

With practice, these techniques will help you confidently connect anywhere, with anyone. By shining light on shared hopes and dreams that are common across humanity, new friends will emerge. Approach every room with an open heart, knowing that kindred spirits await.

ONLINE NETWORKING AND SAFETY

Relationships can develop swiftly online, so both boundless connections and complexities can emerge. While digital platforms exponentially expand your capacity to engage with diverse groups of people, healthy interaction requires ongoing discernment from you. This section illuminates how you can be a responsible digital citizen, protecting your reputation and relationships without forfeiting opportunities. You'll learn wise practices for safeguarding your privacy without sacrificing meaningful access to the online world. Remember: Technology inherently reflects human values coded into its DNA. So, you must model the spirit of the community you wish to see replicated virtually. Always lead with empathy and integrity and be accountable for mistakes. You'll make progress through bold, compassionate experimentation and commitment. If you turn your attention to aligning innovation with conscience, promising pathways will appear, leading technology toward its highest purpose— bringing people together.

The Virtual Handshake

Your online presence shapes people's opinions of your judgment and character. Post meaningful content that spreads positivity. Reply to comments respectfully. Follow the terms of service carefully. Establish alert systems to monitor online mentions for prompt reputation management. Pause before posting emotionally charged content.

Find Your People

Seek niche forums and groups that reflect your authentic passions. Contribute knowledgeably while learning cultural norms. Build trust through consistent engagement that adds value. Subscribe to diverse high-quality channels that curate specialized knowledge. Share your personal experiences that relate to the community dialogue. Reference offline networking contacts who align with your digital interests.

Mind Your (Digital) Manners

Take note of the etiquette conventions involved in online conversations. Reply supportively to user questions. When appropriate, credit your sources. Disagree politely when necessary. Beware of unintended tones that can arise from brevity. Allow others space to correct previous statements without shame. Report abusive behaviors privately to maintain community standards. Welcome newcomers warmly then guide them gently toward constructive participation.

Craft Your Profile

Profiles display your professionalism and intellect that are aligned with audience values. Accurately highlight your achievements, skills, and specializations. Link only to reputable sources. Refresh your content steadily. Showcase any certifications from credentialed institutions and test scores upon permission. Embed reputable media features discussing your innovations. Restrict access selectively to control how your profile appears across audiences.

Join the Conversation

Share knowledge and helpful resources. Pose thoughtful discussion questions. Tag relevant members to widen your reach. Align your offline relationship-building with savvy online networking for well-rounded connections. Form new subgroups when exciting tangents arise that you want to explore further. Facilitate introductions between members with mutual interests.

The digital landscape allows unprecedented access to worldwide support if you navigate it responsibly. You can build your influence through consistent contribution. Soon, your reputation will come knocking. Leave each forum better than you found it through diligent moderation and leadership.

MANAGING ONLINE RELATIONSHIPS

Online interactions differ from in-person in speed, anonymity, and lack of nonverbal cues. This can tend to amplify misunderstandings, but it also allows you to have more control in presenting yourself. This is how your personas can emerge. However, this anonymity can sometimes breed cruelty by reducing empathy and accountability. To be digitally savvy, you must model ethical standards for online conduct. Progress will follow conscience.

Set Boundaries

In your online conversations, establish mutually acceptable response times to prevent unrealistic demands. Tell others your comfort level for discussing certain topics. Always request consent before you shift your tone or try to have a deeper conversation. Be aware that technology can also facilitate unwanted over-access. Schedule designated "no notification" hours for uninterrupted productivity or self-care. Reply once daily during busy times when it's harder to connect. You can always renegotiate these terms when needed.

Avoid Pitfalls

Beware of predators who create false personas to exploit vulnerabilities. Verify individuals independently before you deepen your connection. Meet first in public settings if you are transitioning online bonds to in-person interactions. Also, recognize technology's capacity to obscure people's intentions. Consult trusted adults regarding questionable behaviors if you are unsure of how to proceed. Trust your instincts when you feel the warning of something being too good to be true. Prioritize face-to-face meetings early if you are seeking romantic prospects.

Assess Authenticity

Make sure someone's online persona and actual demonstrated character are the same. Pay more attention to what people do than what they say. Having patience will allow the truth to reveal itself through subtle cracks in curated facades. Notice whose posts elicit joy or inspiration versus comparison or FOMO. Make note of your emotional responses to each interaction. You may have initial judgments, but gathering data over time can help you determine someone's true character.

Guard Privacy

Limit the personal information you share with unknown sources. Utilize security settings that restrict content from unknown contacts. You can also periodically search your name online to monitor any details that might be exposed. Report impersonation accounts or harassment promptly. Establish Google alerts that deliver reputation notifications. You can even compartmentalize the platforms you use for different facets of your life.

While online forums can expand your social access immensely, you need to gain the wisdom it takes to balance your online and offline relationships. Trust actions first, then words. Verify people independently before you disclose anything about yourself. Set clear boundaries around your availability. With these safeguards, you can nurture online relationships with the same care, accountability, and nuance as those cultivated offline.

Understand Cybersecurity for Social Networks

Cybersecurity refers to protecting devices, services, and networks from unauthorized access or attack. As social and professional life integrates online, these basic precautions safeguard reputations. Enable two-factor authentication on your important logins. Have your parents help you install comprehensive antivirus software with auto updates and establish backup protocols for valued digital assets.

Guard Personal Data

Limit sharing your birthday, address, phone, school, and workplace details online. This can facilitate identity theft or stalking. Utilize the strongest privacy settings on your profiles. Periodically review each platform for new exposures. Remove accounts that you no longer use. Never share passwords or PINs except with trusted adults.

Address Cyberbullying

Ignore or block offensive accounts when possible. Report sustained harassment to platforms and adults. Offer emotional support offline within your supportive communities. Document evidence of online abuse by taking screenshots in case an investigation becomes necessary. Don't engage with trolls online; this gives them power. Mute them and move on. Cultivate your self-confidence to strengthen your resilience.

Practice Safe Sharing

Always post responsibly. What you do online today can have echoes years later with unintended audiences. Pause before tagging friends who may want control over their privacy. Fact check before spreading potential misinformation. Reflect sincerely on what motivates your sharing—is it service or ego? Consider how social media can create unhealthy comparisons. Focus your attention more on real-life joy offline.

Seek Help

Many platforms have tools that facilitate guarding data and reporting issues. If necessary, consult legal resources if harassment escalates. Support hotlines can assist you in processing bullying trauma. Bookmark emergency resource pages for quick access if needed. Discuss concerns with older mentors or trusted adults who have experience navigating similar dilemmas. Prevent ongoing pain by reporting early-stage violations.

While cybersecurity requires some vigilance, take heart. Our shared humanity still whispers beneath the noise if we listen. Be the voice of hope. Monitor online spaces vigilantly but contribute focused on positivity, not fear or judgment.

CASE STUDY: SARAH

Sarah was an active user on PlantLoversForum.com, an online community for plant and gardening enthusiasts.

She enjoyed connecting with fellow hobbyists around the world to share photos, tips, and advice about plants. Sarah spent hours daily conversing on forum threads and formed friendships with several regular members over months.

SimonGrowsBestRoses was a prominent user who posted gorgeous photos of rare rose varieties. He and Sarah bonded over their shared rose gardening struggles and messaged extensively. Six months after meeting online, Simon asked if Sarah was interested in a romantic relationship. Sarah declined politely, hoping to remain forum friends.

Unfortunately, Simon turned venomous, insulting Sarah publicly and sending abusive messages. Sarah was devastated and stopped using the forum for months. However, the forum moderator banned Simon, so Sarah returned, feeling supported by other members.

The incident made Sarah institute boundaries about sharing personal information like photos or locations to protect her privacy. It also underscored the importance of assessing digital relationships on demonstrated character over time rather than charm, which takes discernment.

Nonetheless, Sarah continues benefiting from the forum community for plant advice while avoiding divulging identifying details. With reasonable safeguards, she balances the forum's knowledge, sharing advantages against potential risks. The experience taught difficult but important lessons about navigating online social platforms mindfully.

WRAPPING UP...

As you build bonds through understanding and expand your social network, certain complexities arise. Where people gather, subtle hierarchies and social dynamics inevitably emerge. However, with patience and care, you can learn to navigate this complex territory.

The connections that enable support and unity can also produce status structures that impact how you are perceived and treated. In the next chapter, we'll explore the origins and ethics of social stratification and how undeserved advantages can unfairly concentrate influence and disadvantage vulnerable groups.

As with digital spaces, we must enter social hierarchies and consider how to transform unhealthy power imbalances into more equitable participation through moral courage and wisdom. With compassion and discernment, we can structure interactions and institutions to bring out the best in human dignity, not the worst impulses. When people feel equally empowered, cooperation unfolds. As friends and allies, we must model the spirit of community we wish to create.

5

MASTERING SOCIAL MEDIA

Teens spend an average of over three hours daily immersed in social media's potent influence—that's more time spent online than with friends in person (Riehm et al., 2019). As innovation races on exponentially infusing technology into identity formation, "Social media is about sociology and psychology more than technology," Brian Solis astutely warns. This section offers compass points for navigating turbulent digital waters. You'll find strategies for managing screen habits and unlocking the promise of social platforms while sidestepping the accompanying perils. When the online world is aligned with conscience, promising headway unfolds. Insight can connect across divides and awaken movements. Simply avoiding the online world cannot shelter coming generations from these emerging realities. We must create space for nuance and care instead of rigid control. We can stay rooted in humanity's heartbeat while embracing the complexity ahead. There is wisdom to be revealed if we proceed together courageously into unknown terrains of conscience and community.

Let's look ahead to capture advice and lessons on how to balance healthy digital citizenship with well-being in an increasingly virtual age that requires savvier navigation. Our shared future reflects priorities and dreams seeded now through mentorship, education, and modeling uplifting ethics. This is the responsibility of us all.

SOCIAL MEDIA LITERACY

Social technologies permeate daily life, so skillfully navigating digital spaces is vital for teens seeking healthy connections online. Beyond platforms that facilitate identity experiments or fleeting fame obsessions lies communication potential that serves individual fulfillment and collective uplift. This section illuminates the pathways for empowered participation in the virtual cultures that are unfolding around us all. You will learn wise practices for positively managing your social media personas across rising apps while avoiding toxicity. You'll see how you can create ripples of good by intentionally crafting content that brings more light, not noise, into the information ecosystem. Lasting influence arises not through popularity nor provocation but nuanced truth-telling and compassion. Our shared future reflects the dreams seeded now in tiny acts of courage and care.

Understanding Platforms

Popular social media platforms like Instagram, TikTok, YouTube, and Snapchat each have unique cultures. Instagram focuses on visual sharing; TikTok short videos; YouTube longer commentary; and Snapchat short-lived messaging. Choose platforms that suit your interests—photography, current events, gaming, etc. Stay savvy about emerging app trends influenced by celebrity use or algorithm changes that impact visibility. Update your settings to control your data privacy as new features arise. Be mindful that different apps invite different posting styles. Balance your personal branding across accounts. Before sharing, carefully consider what aspects of your identity to cultivate for varying audiences. Posting with intention can prevent future regrets. Monitor the time you spend online and avoid excessive digital entanglement at the expense of living your real life.

Creating Content

If you're interested in creating content online, identify your audience and goals. Craft captions and use relevant hashtags to reach aligned followers without spamming. Show your personality while upholding your values. Visually appealing images and snappy editing keep viewers engaged. Post consistently one to two times weekly without overwhelming your followers' feeds. Promote audience participation via question prompts. Build community by showcasing user-generated content. Monitor insights and fine-tune approaches. If you have the opportunity, collaborate with influencers or brands through sponsorships. Remember to fuel your creativity by logging off periodically and seeking inspiration in the real world. Soon, you'll have fresh perspectives.

Understanding Digital Media Literacy

Carefully consider content permanence before you post. What you share will never disappear entirely. Verify the validity of information before reposting. Credit inspiration sources. Ask your friends for consent before tagging them online. Diffuse digital drama through offline conversations, not public feuds. Be a model of high online standards. Promote media literacy by educating your peers on copyright, privacy rights, and source-checking tips. Don't get sucked into the popularity contest that compares likes and other metrics. Measure your influence through real-life impact instead.

With self-awareness and empathy guiding your online activity, you can create promising connections where users uplift each other through creative expression. Honor the personal experiences of others without exploiting them for reactions. Validate diverse voices and work to find common ground.

THE IMPACT OF SOCIAL MEDIA ON RELATIONSHIPS

As virtual relationships increasingly permeate social life, particularly for digitally immersed teens, both profound connections and troubling comparisons can arise. This section offers compass points to navigate the currents of peer pressure that can threaten your self-esteem. You'll learn how to distinguish superficial ties from bonds that nurture your highest self. We'll learn how to chart passageways that uphold wisdom on social platforms. When technology isolates rather than uplifts, its purpose rings hollow and is lost chasing algorithms without conscience. Yet, courageous voices can model virtue by choosing community over vanity. Our digital footsteps can trace toward togetherness as friends or guides lighting darkened tunnels until all find belonging.

Fostering Real Connections

Social platforms should complement rather than replace offline interactions. Work to transform online connections into fuller in-person friendships. Sustain old ties by messaging those who may now be distant. Customize your visibility settings and self-disclosures to balance openness with privacy. Seek consent before posting about the personal moments of others. Clarify context to reduce misinterpreting brief messages. Schedule offline catch-ups to nurture friendships. Set boundaries around digital availability to prevent overuse. Monitor whether your social media use uplifts or drains your energy over time. Reassess your habits and adjust them when necessary.

Social Media and Peer Pressure

Fear of missing out (FOMO) breeds unhealthy social comparisons online. Recognize that filtered images often misrepresent reality. When you comment, do so with genuine support, not envy. Disable notifications briefly if you find yourself compulsively checking your status. Politely decline viral dare chains that could risk your safety or values. Report concerning challenges discreetly to a trusted adult. Model positive behaviors that uplift marginalized voices over petty gossip. Your integrity matters more than likes. Discuss pitfalls and ground rules for social media participation with your family to establish shared values. Study how technology intentionally fosters addiction through dopamine hits. This media literacy will enable you to make smart decisions online.

The Role of Influencers

Influencers profoundly impact the purchase decisions and worldviews of their followers. Yet, this fame can come with the risk of corrupted ethics and exploitation. Encourage the creators you follow to uphold community good over division or superficiality. Support independent voices over big brand promotions. Understand the difference between content that aims to enlighten or merely sell you something. Many wise role models out there are worth following. Follow local influencers who build personal, authentic connections.

While social platforms can promise both connections and pressures, you can find fulfillment by consciously connecting. Focus your interactions on mutual understanding and collective uplift. Monitor whether tools claiming connectivity breed isolation or genuine bonds, then seek balance.

DIGITAL WELLNESS AND SAFETY

As innovation races onward, screens have become part of our routines, so it's vital to navigate the promising possibilities and mitigate the accompanying perils. This section offers compass points to chart passageways through the turbulent digital waters that uphold humanity's highest welfare. You'll find strategies for securing data and reducing device dependence so your clarity and connection are not eclipsed by speed's dazzling glare. We must nurture wisdom in applying tools and judiciously monitor safety. When aligned with conscience, promising headway unfolds in the digital landscape—insight connects distant hearts, ideas ignite movements, and voices unite commanding justice. Our shared future will reflect the priorities instilled today in laws both legal and natural, upholding what it means to be human. So, let's learn to lead with care and courage.

Manage Screen Time

You can limit recreational screen time through parental controls and monitoring tools. Set usage goals to reduce your screen time gradually. Learn to recognize excessive digital immersion symptoms such as isolation or compulsion. Schedule device-free activities and enjoy real-world engagement. Craft media diets that balance online and offline nourishment. Monitor changes in your mood, sleep, and academics to gauge screen time's impact holistically. Restrict overnight access to devices to facilitate healthy sleep hygiene. Nurture friendships through shared hobbies and dedicated listening.

Address Cyberbullying

Online harassment can inflict profound damage. Report sustained bullying to platforms and authorities. Comfort victims by spreading community awareness over blaming. Discuss healthy digital norms with your family, friends, and any organizations you are a part of. Promote peer modeling to uplift marginalized voices. If you can, fund counseling that aids anxiety and depression triggered by online abuse. Weave connection to cushion trauma's blow and remind those who are struggling of their inherent worth.

Protect Privacy

Guard your personal information by sharing only the required details. Restrict visibility settings on all your accounts. Verify the legitimacy of a site before inputting any data. Cybercrime threatens us all, so spread savviness about online scams. While screens promise both bridges and barriers, wisdom will guide your way if you listen.

CASE STUDY: SANJAY

Sanjay was an aspiring musician who enjoyed connecting with friends and fans through Instagram and TikTok. He often posted covers of popular songs and built a following of over 50,000

people. Sanjay felt pressure to constantly create content, improve his online image, and respond to followers. Over time, Sanjay became preoccupied with monitoring his metrics and reading comments for hours daily. His mood declined when posts underperformed. Sanjay lost interest in school, friends, and even creating music as producing content consumed all available time. He increasingly isolated himself from human connections and became absorbed in manufactured online validation. Sanjay's creativity also suffered by focusing on popularity rather than meaningful self-expression. His mental and emotional health deteriorated under the weight of unrealistic expectations.

Noticing changes, Sanjay's parents discussed their concerns. They helped Sanjay recognize that he was falling into unhealthy social media obsession rather than using platforms for meaningful connections. Together, they established boundaries, including no phones during dinner and breaks between posting. Sanjay took up volleyball again to shift his focus back to personal passions offline. He scheduled performances at local venues to translate online fans into real-world friendships. While still creating content, Sanjay sought balance and authenticity over chasing metrics. He reports feeling happier and more creatively fulfilled. Sanjay's story inspired friends to reflect on their technology habits, too. His vulnerability strengthened bonds and expanded awareness of digital wellness.

Sanjay's story reveals the importance of monitoring your digital habits. With compassion and wisdom, you can work with your family and friends to avoid obsessive social media use and instead unlock technology's potential to ignite purpose and community. Ongoing dialogue and balance will help you learn self-regulation.

WRAPPING UP...

While social technologies unlock immense potential for human connection, face-to-face interactions remain vital for your holistic well-being. As you learn to balance meaningful digital engagement with self-care and real-world community, still greater growth unfolds through courageous in-person vulnerability. When people truly see and hear each other deeply, defenses soften and allow wisdom to emerge.

KEEPING THE GAME ALIVE

"Children are the living messages we send to a time we will not see."

Life's a big adventure, and guess what? People who share their goodness without waiting for a pat on the back tend to have the happiest, most extraordinary adventures. So, let's make our adventure together super special.

I've got a tiny yet mighty favor to ask...

Have you ever helped someone just because? Maybe someone a bit like you, back when everything was big and confusing? Someone eager to make a mark, hungry for a guiding light, but lost in the dark?

Our big dream is to make *Social Skills for Teens Decoded* a flashlight for every teen wandering in the maze of growing up. Everything we do, every word we write, sparks from this dream. And to turn this dream into a super-bright reality, we need to reach... well...every teen out there!

And here's where you, yes YOU, become our superhero. Most people judge a book by its cover (and its reviews). So, here's my superhero request on behalf of a teen out there who you've never met:

Please light up their path by leaving a shining review for this book.

Your superpower doesn't cost a dime and takes less than a magic minute, but it can change another teen's world. Your review might help...

One more teen finds their voice.

One more dreamer chasing their dream.

One more future leader takes their first step.

One more brave heart stands up to a bully.

One more bright mind understands the puzzle of emotions.

Ready to sprinkle some of your magic? Here's how – and it's quicker than a blink!

Just scan the QR code below to cast your spell of kindness:

If your heart feels warm thinking about helping a fellow teen you've never seen, you're absolutely our kind of hero. Welcome to the club, the circle of unseen superheroes.

I'm super excited to guide you to:

- Stand tall with unshakable confidence.
- Weave the web of deepest friendships.
- Master the art of chatting, both in the digital world and face-to-face.
- Dodge the tricky traps of peer pressure and cyberbullies.

- Ride the rollercoaster of feelings like a pro.
- Explore the maze of modern friendships and social media like a fearless explorer.

These skills and secrets await you in the pages ahead, and you will be wowed by the journey we've planned!

Thank you from every corner of my heart. Now, let's dive back into our big adventure!

- Your biggest cheerleader, Yudelkis Murray

P.S. - Little secret: Sharing a treasure makes you a treasure! If you feel this book is a gem, why not share it with another teen? Pass the light forward.

6

HANDLING CONFLICT AND REJECTION

At age 30, Stephen King finally completed the novel *Carrie*, though he was initially rejected more than 30 times. The story explores isolation and revenge following relentless high school bullying. When published, the book launched his career.

As Stephen King demonstrated through perseverance and transforming rejection into a massive success, human character and purpose are revealed as much from conflicts weathered as a smooth ascent. Let's explore tools to find growth opportunities within disappointing failures or strained relationships. If engaged consciously, these tools will help you glean wisdom and improve your approach. You'll find stories and strategies modeling integrity that gradually sway skeptics and discover tactics for turning tension into a teacher.

UNDERSTANDING CONFLICT

When people come together, disagreements naturally arise from different perspectives. However, conflict doesn't have to become

hostile if it is handled constructively. Skillfully addressed, clashes can crack open portals to richer understanding that would otherwise be obscured by defensive reactions. This section shows pathways to travel courageously through dissent toward mutual wisdom. You'll find practical tools and insights to build your self-awareness, defuse emotional reactivity, and elevate communication. These tools can gradually transform fiery conflicts into light. Once people feel truly heard and understood, their guarded facades will yield to showcase our shared humanity. Common ground can reconnect and revive strained relationships. With openness, empathy, and care, we can untangle social knots into a community again made whole. So, when storms arise, look inward, breathe deeply, and then lead the way. Progress follows peace, not force. Healing begins when one heart listens and barriers fall as we uncover the fundamental goodness in us all.

The Nature of Conflict

Conflict naturally arises in human relationships. It's understandable, given that we all have varied perspectives and needs. Rather than an inherently negative force, conflict presents growth opportunities when it is handled constructively. Open communication and willingness to understand facilitate working through issues. You can learn to embrace conflict proactively as a portal for increased closeness and wisdom.

Teens commonly experience conflicts around privacy, chores, money, responsibilities, relationships, beliefs, or values. Whatever your source of conflict, you can accept differing expectations as inevitable. You can also demonstrate accountability by addressing problems proactively. Clarify agreements early to establish healthy boundaries around trust and autonomy that are appropriate for your age. Renegotiate the terms when needed.

Anatomy of Conflict

Conflicts escalate in cycles beginning from a trigger, rising tensions, climax confrontation, then gradual de-escalation toward resolution. You can observe this pattern mindfully rather than reacting defensively. Reflect on your usual conflict style, which could be avoiding, accommodating, or competing. Interrupt escalation early by voicing your grievances calmly and focusing discussions on issues not people. Breathe before responding if your emotions are heightened.

Emotions in Conflict

Strong emotions—such as anger, hurt, or fear—often overlay conflicts. However, productive resolutions often follow when issues and needs take center stage over running narratives. Listen generously and own your true feelings using "I" statements. Allow space for emotions to settle before responding. You can even schedule a set time to voice any resentments accumulated over minor unaddressed incidents. Then, you can use the opportunity to clean the slate with forgiveness.

With mindfulness and courage, conflict can illuminate opportunities for relational growth through new understanding. Lead compassionately and see the human behind hardened narratives. You'll find progress through a steadfast commitment to hearing all voices until unity is restored. Shine light where shadows obscure; truth and reconciliation heal.

Communicating During Conflict

Effective conflict resolution requires open, respectful communication focused on understanding all perspectives. Listen first rather than immediately voicing your stance. Clarify what other people are saying by asking thoughtful questions. Own your true emotions and needs with "I feel" statements. Find shared goals. Establish group guidelines that value mutually respectful dialogue. Share any triggered feelings without assigning blame. You make more progress by being curious than by accusing.

Active Listening

Initially, suspend your judgment, interruptions, or problem-solving. Reflect on key points to demonstrate genuine curiosity for their viewpoint. This builds trust and de-escalates tension. It is easier to make progress when people feel heard. Paraphrase content and emotional undertones to ensure you've understood correctly. Allow silence for reflection and to gather thoughts between statements. Listening intently unpacks complexity.

Staying Calm

High emotions often fan the flames of conflict through reactive body language, interrupting, or accusations. Monitor your internal state and make a conscious effort to breathe slowly. Take pauses to release physical tension before responding. Go for walks to incorporate movement into emotional processing. Write down your feelings privately before discussing them when you are extremely triggered.

You cannot demand that others remain calm unless you model self-control first.

Finding Common Ground

Discuss disputes in issue-focused terms. You could even outline each party's underlying motivations and constraints. Uncover your shared hopes through compassionate dialogue to reconcile seemingly opposed positions into mutually acceptable agreements. Identify how each person's needs might align. Come up with solutions that accommodate both perspectives. Revisit the terms of your agreements if they fail to address ongoing conflicts.

Practice Resolving Conflict

You can have your friends or a trusted adult role-play scenarios that address typical teen disputes, such as chores or allowance. Take turns articulating each perspective and listening carefully. Brainstorm win-win compromises that respect the core needs of both sides. With practice, you can strengthen these skills and learn to lead compassionately. Consider performing skits that demonstrate unhealthy versus healthy conflict engagement styles. You can discuss your observations after and act on what you learn.

When conflicts ignite, do your best to move toward not away from each other. If you remain open, you will be able to find a solution. Darkness cannot drive out darkness, only light can. Afterward, reflect on the conflict and use it for self-improvement.

Knowing When to Walk Away

There are times when walking away from a relationship is the wisest choice. Assess openly whether both parties remain willing to understand each other's perspectives and revisit agreements. Recognize when ego or entitlement prevents collaborative conflict resolution. If patterns of manipulation, passive aggression, violence, or untreated mental health issues emerge, consider disengaging temporarily or permanently, prioritizing your safety first. Communicate your boundaries and what conditions would warrant ending the relationship. You can also request help from a family member, trusted adult, or counselor before abandoning hope. If your declared limits are breached, walking away with courage and integrity can become the healthiest decision.

Coping Afterward

Process lingering hurt by acknowledging your unmet expectations and releasing resentment. Journal, exercise, or consult supporters to help you gain closure. Focus your energy on enriching relationships and nourishing your growth. Allow yourself to mourn losing once meaningful connections to honor authentic grief. Be gentle with shortcomings—both your own and the other person's.

Seeking Support

Trusted friends and professionals can help you objectively determine when healthy conflict resolution proves impossible. Reporting abuse shows courage and wisdom. You deserve environments where all voices hold equal weight. Cultivate diverse social groups, including mentorships that specifically support your major life goals. Your family, peers, organizations, and specialist input can provide holistic sounding boards.

Learning From the Experience

Reflect constructively on your conflict triggers and style. Consider the roles you played in escalating tensions. Forgive your inner critic. Set intentional goals for improving your communication habits that thoughtfully apply the deeper lessons you've learned from hard experiences. Once the initial pain has been tempered by the passage of time, you can gain wisdom. Review past arguments and adjust your foundations before future tests arise. We all stumble along the path, but getting up and giving grace allows us to make progress.

With courage, we speak the truth, and we can then stand unmoving in our worth; with grace, we hold space for growth. When doors close, we can find new passages where belonging waits unseen just ahead if we walk onward. The strongest hearts endure isolation bravely, never growing hardened in freedom's name.

DEALING WITH REJECTION

The piercing sting of rejection inevitably reaches even the most seasoned hearts when friends pull away, romantic interest dissolves, or hard-won opportunities suddenly slip through grasping fingers. Sometimes, our pride may reflexively unleash self-protective impulses to minimize our hurt by disengaging. However, by reframing rejection as an expected norm on the passage toward self-realization—rather than a personalized attack defining our worth—we can find productive ways forward. This section provides strategies and stories to strengthen your resilience in the face of rejection and convert temporary failure into lessons that will help prepare you for the future. Within collapse often comes seeds of reconstruction; inside loss lies gain if we walk on with heads held high. We can use life's rejections to reorient our approach to be wiser and more assured.

THE REALITY OF REJECTION

Despite our best efforts, everyone will inevitably experience rejection—a friend moving away, a crush politely declining, or a job application being denied. While disappointing, you can frame rejection as an expected part of life rather than a reflection of your self-worth. This mindset will strengthen your resilience in the face of uncertainty. Study public figures who were once rejected before great success. Recognize that no personal journey unfolds without obstacles. Your capacity to overcome adversity defines your character.

Learning From Rejection

Constructive feedback can also provide growth opportunities disguised as temporary failure. Ask trusted advisors to analyze scenarios honestly and highlight areas where you could improve. Use these critiques thoughtfully, balancing self-compassion with accountability to cultivate grit. Unpacking rejection in this way can help you discover overlooked blind spots that need to be addressed. However, weigh any external critiques against your internal wisdom; you will find truth in both. Each failure sows seeds for eventual blooming success.

Bouncing Back

Recharge your spirits and confidence through self-care practices before re-entering the arena. Visualize the future victory you will have through your diligent effort. Support groups model that by learning adaptable skills, we don't have to internalize rejection as permanent sentences that dictate our capabilities. They are temporary setbacks on our journey to realizing greater purposes. When doors close today, more open, and they bear the fruits of wisdom gained through the storms we've weathered. Channel the frustration of rejection into fuel that drives your goals. Allow time for emotional recovery from the pain's sting, then rededicate your focus.

NAVIGATING GROUP CONFLICTS AND PEER PRESSURE

Groups provide a sense of belonging, but they can also create unhealthy social pressures (de Guzman, 2020). This section offers tips for handling cliques, gossip, and conflicts. You'll learn to stand up to peer pressure while also bringing people together.

Make sure everyone is treated fairly during disputes. Build confidence in your values when you face pushback. Find supportive friends who celebrate your real self. Be a role model of integrity and compassion online, too. Words can unite or divide us. Promote media literacy to handle cyberbullying and misinformation maturely. The goal is to create spaces where we understand each other despite different backgrounds. Set an example by staying thoughtful in heated moments. Progress happens when we lead with empathy first.

Group Dynamics and Conflict

Group conflicts are uniquely complex and require balancing the needs of individuals, relationships, and overall cohesion. Leaders must address issues fairly and hear all perspectives. You can de-escalate rising tensions through respectful communication that is focused on mutual understanding. Compassionate mediation that focuses on shared values can result in creative compromises. Establish clear guidelines and accountability systems to resolve disputes constructively. Our collective future depends on learning to address tensions maturely.

Standing Up to Peer Pressure

Learn to recognize when peer pressure manifests through teasing, gossip, exclusion, or encouragement toward questionable activities. Build your assertiveness skills by firmly expressing your boundaries while avoiding self-righteousness. Identify friends who validate your constructive choices. You can sustain your inner integrity and lasting self-respect through standing up for your values, not through the temporary validation of false conformity. Analyze the anxiety that might be driving your need for peer approval beyond healthy belonging. Cultivate diverse friend groups to avoid fixation on particular acceptance sources. Honor your authentic callings regardless of external recognition.

Cyber Conflicts and Peer Pressure

Online forums can breed hyper-criticism and tribal conformity. Set healthy permissions on messaging access to prevent any unrelenting pressures. Report abusive cyber-bullying while consoling distress compassionately. Model positive digital citizenship. Wisdom advocates balancing screen time with real-world community. Promote media literacy and strengthen users in discerning misinformation spread unwittingly. Forge groups that uplift marginalized voices and human rights education.

Progress unfolds gradually when you live your values consistently despite trials that test your commitment. All teens struggle to stay anchored in a greater purpose, but you can always choose conscience over popularity and coherence over chaos, allowing truth to gather fragmented pieces into a purposeful movement. Lead by lifting others beyond the limits of their vision. There is light ahead once we walk beyond the pull of lower instincts that are still inevitably within us all.

CASE STUDY: MAYA

Maya switched schools before sixth grade. She felt anxious to make new friends. While kind kids existed, a trio of seemingly popular girls excluded outsiders from activities. Maya tried to relate to them through shared music interests and fashion, but she endured frequent ridicule when her attempts failed, intensifying her isolation.

Feeling depressed, Maya considered changing herself to fit in but confided her dilemma to compassionate parents and friends from her previous school. They reminded Maya that cruelty and gossip reflected poorly on bullies rather than intrinsic flaws. Maya practiced self-affirmations to regain confidence and joined school clubs to cultivate genuine connections.

Though initially hurt by rejection, Maya focused her energy on lifting other shy students through random acts of kindness. Eventually, the lead bully who fueled exclusion apologized, and perceiving Maya's authenticity, asked for a second chance at friendship.

Maya's brave vulnerability in the face of conflict softened the harder hearts over time.

Maya's story demonstrates that while rejection stings in the moment, resilience and integrity can gradually transform strained relationships into a thriving community. Progress unfolds when we lead with love.

WRAPPING UP...

Navigating conflict and rejection are essential skills for relating deeply across the spectrum of human experience. Mastering strategies that turn discord into growth equips you for leadership roles that cultivate collective potential.

The pages ahead reveal timeless insights on discerning authentic leadership traits centered on integrity and service. You'll learn the hallmarks of ethical leadership, as well as the pitfalls that undermine morale and trust when unchecked bias creeps in. Cultivating self-awareness helps ensure that we empower others as guides, mentors, and decision-makers dedicated to community advancement.

When called to steward responsibilities for groups or institutions, progress follows principles, elevating all members' dignity, not just select demographics. Modeling courage through controversy today plants seeds that will inspire others toward destiny's highest purposes tomorrow.

7
THE ART OF PERSUASION

"The best way to persuade people is with your ears, by listening to them."

— DEAN RUSH

The wise counsel of former Secretary of State Dean Rusk teaches us that beyond brute political force lies power through truly understanding other people's hearts and channeling collective goodwill. In this chapter, we'll explore the dynamic art of influence through ethical means.

You'll learn tools founded on integrity that compellingly realign perspectives, not through manipulation but through expanding mutual understanding. When people feel respected, vibrant movements emerge bonded by inspiration, not

intimidation. Much as persuasion
focuses singularly on receptive minds, leadership rallies cooperative
hearts to uplift and unify purpose.

Lasting positive influence comes from appealing to conscience, not
just fleeting emotions. We must stand accountable, carefully questioning and listening for wisdom. Progress happens gradually when
someone bravely and compassionately speaks up about injustice.
This can help people see a shared responsibility to fix problems that
they could not see before. It brings people together instead of
dividing them.

FOUNDATIONS OF PERSUASION

Persuasion involves the strategic use of communication to influence
people's opinions, motivations, or behaviors. Beyond coercion,
ethical persuasion aligns viewpoints with underlying values by
appealing to logic, emotion, or authority, which can create voluntary
change.

History's most enduring voices strategically shaped narratives and
turned the tides over time by understanding intrinsic motivators.
Manipulation that distorts truth violates integrity and threatens
progress. Examine persuasive messaging impartially first. Does the
means justify the ends morally?

Persuasion can calmly and subtly permeate lives... or it can manipu-
late through distortion. We must self-reflect continuously. Why is
someone trying to persuade us? Why are we trying to persuade
someone else? Truth sustains positive influence, while misinformation can cause dysfunction. When aligned with conscience focused
on real societal advancement, even perceived enemies can become

allies over time as light permeates darkness gently. The choice remains with persuaders: unite or divide.

The Psychology Behind Persuasion

Robert Cialdini's influential research outlines the universal principles that drive human behavior, which can be exploited by savvy persuaders (Cialdini, 2007). People can feel obligated to return favors after receiving support. Scarcity can pressure people to act when they think opportunities are passing them by. People often simplify complex dynamics by creating mental shortcuts, which makes them vulnerable to biases and detached from the truth. This reveals intricate social or political realities.

Facts alone rarely change people's perspectives. The deeper drivers that inspire conviction and sacrifice are threats to security, belonging, identity, or justice. Persuasive messages align meaning with underlying core values and concerns.

Without dependability, social contracts start to come apart. Claims of competency demand repeated proof, while character reflects through integrity that maintains cohesive relationships and hierarchies. Humility gains influence by seeking counsel from others.

We make progress by persuading through principle, not just passion. When we appeal first to hearts and minds through genuine goodwill, we avoid the forced hand that secures superficial gain. People support what they help build. We align with a call to a purpose that sustains a vision greater than ourselves. Where there is division, plant seeds that redeem broken ties. The future rests in how ideas take root through wisdom—or manipulation—today.

Persuasion Techniques

We can establish credibility through experience or integrity to earn the trust of our audience. Logos appeals to people rationally and builds arguments that are focused on facts, data, and logic. Pathos appeals to people emotionally and can inspire hope, anger, patriotism, justice, or other internal motivators. Combining both types of persuasion can adapt messages and maximize their impact across diverse groups of people.

Stories captivate by drawing listeners into relatable narratives that are anchored in communal values and aspirations. Statistical reports scarcely inspire sacrifice, yet anecdotal tales rally support through felt connection. Craft tension-building scenarios that can be resolved through collective participation. Let protagonists model the desired mindsets and actions.

Visuals can help clarify complex dynamics through simple infographics, photographs, and videos. Allow visuals to argue on your behalf elegantly and condense multidimensional issues into concise media that leaves a lasting impression.

Framing can help set context through precise language, supporting the strengths of your position and the weaknesses of alternatives. Favorable first impressions transfer to positive assumptions, thwarting counter perspectives. Define issues on your terms, dismissing the legitimacy of critiques that may be out of hand.

With practice, we can hone the techniques that elevate discussion from being combative to inspiring. We can show that we are open and still stand firm in our principles. We can listen for faint signals from even the fiercest critics that indicate there are common hopes. There is fertile ground for sowing change, and we can plant seeds so everyone prospers.

No matter the reach of our influence, the choice remains: unite or divide, enrich understanding or distort it for ego's gain. Lead wisely; our future depends on the paths we pave today.

PERSUASION IN PRACTICE

Wherever people come together, influence—whether it's subtle or overt—is a natural force that shapes group dynamics and personal decisions. In this section, you'll learn skills to bolster passionate arguments with reason and tap into intrinsic motivations. True influence comes from living by your principles, not just by being passionate. Progress happens by patiently listening, finding common ground, and slowly bringing people together into cooperation. Progress stops if we fail to recognize the humanity in those who oppose us. But when we follow our conscience, we can use discretion either to reveal the truth or sever ties when needed. The future relies on choices that expand freedoms for all, and wise leadership means planting seeds so everyone can flourish.

Persuasion in Relationships

While perceived manipulation damages bonds, skillful influence aligns relationships through win-win conflict resolution. Negotiate needs non-coercively by referencing shared hopes. Ask curious questions to understand and discuss people's objections rather than reacting defensively. Come up with compromises that uphold the core concerns of both parties.

You can creatively gain team buy-in by linking suggestions to the recognized group goals. Then, back them with factual research not just passion. Validate the ideas of others to improve cohesion.

Progress will follow when you replace accusations with collaborative inquiry.

For example, when Robin wanted permission to attend concerts, her cautious father refused, fearing that the venues were unsafe. So, Robin compiled venue safety statistics and procedures, referencing her dad's core concern for her well-being. Addressing his underlying worries through data demonstrated Robin's responsibility. Her father agreed to a trial concert outing, appreciating Robin's initiative.

Lead persuasively through principle, not just passion. Plant seeds in the fertile common ground. That way, understanding can take root and blossom gradually where shadows once loomed. Reveal shared visions through patience and care and resist reactionary threats.

Persuasion in the Digital World

Digital media allows us to personalize niche targeting based on people's browsing behavior, demographics, and personality types. This information is cataloged through data aggregation powered by machine learning. We can leverage multiple formats to increase messaging saturation. Videos can condense complex narratives into a felt experience. When seeking to persuade people online, we can even invest in quality production and distribution through paid boosting, which can secure the reach of our message.

Harnessing Social Media

Influencers show us how viral behaviors through trusted voices drive human behavior. Yet, many of the people we follow peddle warehouse products from questionable manufacturers. These are secured through affiliate deals to earn them income. You have a choice of who you follow on social media. Support creators who uphold community advancement over division or sales.

Authenticity Resonates

Lasting movements gather momentum through grassroots support driven by integrity-based causes that benefit ordinary people—not campaigns that manufacture illusions through bots and fake accounts. We have tools for connection that are unmatched in history, and when we engage in social media responsibly, promising new pathways of connection emerge.

This type of communication can awaken compassion across divides that were once deemed impassable chasms of distance or differences. Truth-rooted communication can guide all who wander home again. So, where there is division, may we plant seeds of reconciliation before the opportunity passes. Soon, another soul will look to you for direction amidst the disarray. Lead first with courage and care.

Persuasion for Social Good

Passion alone scarcely sways public sentiments and can limit the awareness of overlooked injustices. Do your homework about the causes you care about to reinforce your credibility. Outline the scope of the issue with illustrations. Share community voices, which can help you detail the impacts. Align any charitable appeals with supporter values by giving context—suffering elicits empathy, and injustice threatens moral systems. Clearly define incremental policy changes you'd like to see and address root grievances. Show people how they can become protagonists in your cause.

When emotionally conveyed and channeled tactically, speeches drive movements through inspiration. Study body language cues and verbal pacing patterns, which can help you gain the attention of audiences. Record rehearsals to refine your delivery and make it more impactful. These time-tested techniques amplify calls to action and help you plant seeds so everyone can prosper.

Our voices may tremble initially, but being empowered by our purpose can shift cultural tides gradually, then thunderously with organized dedication. There is light ahead once we stand up to claim dignity for marginalized souls. Justice has the momentum to gather fragmented causes into coherent groundswells channeled creatively. Persuasion can pave roads we then march down together.

IMPROVING YOUR COMMUNICATION

Persuasive communication skills develop your authoritative presence through speech clarity, compelling vocal pace variation, strategic pausing, and elimination of verbal ticks. Practice public speaking routinely, then request feedback from your coaches, friends, or other adults to help target areas where you can improve. You can create and implement targeted improvement plans based on constructive critiques.

You can use physical cues to convey your conviction by synchronizing hand gestures, facial expressions, and posture shifts to stress crucial points during delivery. You can even record presentation rehearsals so you can analyze places where you can improve your body language and delivery. Soon, you will exude gravitas and will be able to channel an audience's energy toward your desired goals.

Active listening is the highest art of persuasion. It forges bonds built through communicative presence and attuning to unspoken needs. Master influencers first seek to understand community concerns and dreams before artfully illuminating common ground.

With wisdom, patience, and continuous self-reflection, your persuasive abilities will manifest naturally once your intentions align with equitable growth and collective advancement. When speech elevates, deeds match soaring rhetoric and compassion permeates engagement. Hearts open receptivity to progress. Lead first through courage, empathy, and care.

Overcoming Resistance

You can anticipate critiques proactively by identifying any weaknesses in your logical reasoning. You can use this knowledge to come up with proposed solutions before critics have the opportunity to counter your argument. You can also openly raise and address counterarguments first, which will strengthen your point and help dilute attempts to derail the discussion.

Seek common ground by pointing out shared priorities and values among opposing arguments through non-judgmental questioning. Ask what makes skeptics feel better and use that information to build enough consensus around shared values.

Expect some pushback and understand that universal acceptance is unlikely, even if you feel you have airtight logic. Review any feedback you receive and use it as an opportunity to refine your argument rather than reacting defensively. Not all resistance indicates flaws in your ideas; sometimes, people's minds change slower than visionaries ahead of their era.

Always be prepared to adapt your communication strategies, recognizing that one message or medium may fail to resonate across all groups. Consider varied approaches to meet target groups where they stand through familiar language.

Commit to the long game by studying inspiring speakers who overcame resistance through sustained public persuasion before shifting cultural opinions and policies. Stay persistent yet flexible when you encounter resistance. With relatability, ethicality, and emotional intelligence, communicators can transform hostility into humanity.

Practicing Persuasion Ethically

We can maintain credible influence by being reliable and authentic. We must also learn to acknowledge our limitations and avoid spreading misinformation. Being transparent helps win people's trust.

Allow your audience to maintain their autonomy and support well-reasoned ideas without coercion, deception, or emotional manipulation. You can reframe inconvenient truths but do not omit them. Make sure you have consent before sharing any private details. This allows you to influence ethically.

Create accountability by asking mentors, friends, or family members to highlight ethical blind spots. You can grow by acknowledging areas for moral character improvement. Lasting positive influence flows through principle. Lead first with courage, then empathy and care.

CASE STUDY: JAMAL

As student council president, Jamal aimed to unite his school across racial and social lines. However, an anonymous Instagram account began attacking immigrant students with racist slurs. Tensions boiled over, and fights erupted between marginalized and nationalist groups.

Jamal appealed to the students' shared needs for security and belonging, denouncing the bullying without blame or judgment against any group. He organized a unity rally for justice. However, vandals sabotaged preparations the night before.

Devastated but undeterred, Jamal mobilized volunteers to rebuild damaged infrastructure for the rally launched as scheduled. During his heartfelt speech acknowledging pain on all sides, he appealed to conscience, "When we dehumanize anyone, all humanity suffers." Moved attendees crossed dividing aisles with hugs initiated by the instigators of previous wrongs.

Jamal demonstrated how ethical persuasion uplifts unity where bitterness and paralysis once prevailed. Progress unfolds gradually and then suddenly through small cumulative acts of courage. There is light if we lead together toward seeing shared burdens waiting behind the fear.

WRAPPING UP...

Influence and persuasion are crucial interpersonal skills, yet creating positive change requires moving others to action through effective leadership. The pages ahead will reveal timeless insights guiding the cultivation of wisdom and integrity that transform teams, families, organizations, and movements.

You'll learn foundational principles grounded in service, empowerment, and collective advancement, distinguishing moral authority from egoistic self-aggrandizement. Much like persuasion tends to focus singly on receptive minds, leadership engages hearts cooperatively to uplift everyone.

When we are called to steward the potential in others, progress follows by upholding what lifts all rather than the few. Model virtue through adversity. Shoulder burdens first before asking for sacrifice. Honor each unique voice's gift to drive change.

8

EMPATHY AND EMOTIONAL INTELLIGENCE

"When you show deep empathy toward others, their defensive energy goes down, and positive energy replaces it."

— STEPHEN COVEY

Reflected in the words of Stephen Covey, these pages show emotional intelligence's power to uplift relationships and resolve conflicts by seeing people's humanity.

You'll learn to calmly respond to triggers with patience, address root issues to find the truth, and model personal resilience through self-care. With these tools, you can inspire progress with compassionate leadership. When people feel fully understood, positive change unfolds.

Specifically, you'll discover ways to celebrate team successes, check in one-on-one to sense how people are truly doing, and coach gently versus command. You'll be able to meet confusion with caring support, not rushed advice. Ears matter more than mouths. Growth happens gradually when we lead with courage, empathy, and care.

WHAT IS EMOTIONAL INTELLIGENCE (EI)?

Emotional intelligence (EI) is the ability to understand your emotions and the emotions of others. With emotional intelligence, you can apply sensitivity and adapt thinking and actions for optimal outcomes. Mastering complex inner states and social dynamics is critical for success. Smarts alone cannot guarantee fulfilling lives or relationships. High IQ still misses key skills for managing emotions wisely.

This section shares ways to grow your self-awareness, understand others better, and communicate clearly despite stress. You'll learn how to stay calm, focused, and kind even during difficult times. You'll be able to put passion into positive action without overre-acting and see past first impressions. No one handles pressure perfectly all the time, but the tools here can help defuse tension, heal divisions, and find purpose.

EI Components

Emotional intelligence is made up of several factors:

- Self-awareness involves recognizing your moods, motivation, and impact to guide your behavior.
- Self-regulation means you can maintain composure while managing impulses and stress.

- Motivation helps you channel emotions toward your goals.
- Empathy is the ability to sense others' feelings and to relate to them compassionately.
- Social skills allow you to artfully communicate, influence, and connect diverse personalities.

Each domain requires ongoing cultivation. As your skills strengthen, you'll be able to integrate your capabilities fluidly and respond situationally without a rigid formula.

Assessment and Growth

Many surveys are available that can measure your EI strengths and limitations. Once you know where you need to improve, you can practice techniques such as journaling your mood patterns, deep breathing when you are triggered, and role-playing tricky interpersonal dynamics until responses flow intuitively. Accept occasional stumbles with self-compassion as you continue to do your best. We all struggle sometimes to handle hurt or frustration. What matters most is committing to progress daily. Change starts within before you can transform worlds without.

Managing Emotions

Strategies to manage emotions include deep breathing when triggered, journaling to process feelings privately before responding outwardly, and cognitive restructuring. When possible, reduce triggers and manage stress proactively through self-care. Integrate tools that elevate resilience and restoration holistically over relying on sheer willpower alone.

Mindfulness and Meditation

Regular mindfulness practicing non-judgmental emotional pattern awareness reduces your reactivity, anxiety, and depression while improving your focus and relationship harmony. Even brief sessions have benefits that compound long-term. Allow feelings to arise rather than suppress or escalate. Consider formal meditation, redirecting busy thoughts toward grounded calm. Much like physical health requires proper nutrition and movement, emotional health depends on basic strategies to alleviate excessive volatility.

Emotional Growth Goals

Setting incremental emotional intelligence development goals helps you make situations that were previously triggering easier to navigate. Journal your progress to manage your responses. You can also request feedback to assess improvements others have noticed. Soon, you'll form automatic habits and will be able to defuse stressors that previously may have derailed you. We all struggle sometimes, but what matters most is committing to uplifting communication through accountability, patience, and care.

Motivation Tied to Emotions: Emotions Drive Goals

Emotional patterns reveal our deeper passions and values. Use self-awareness to set meaningful personal goals that tap into your authentic motivations. Understand what truly drives you. Notice where your enthusiasm and resistance emerge, observing life rhythms and activities. Does your mood lift or deplete around particular environments or conversations? This insight allows you to redirect your energy toward fulfillment.

Positivity Fuels Motivation

Positive emotions—like hope, interest, and pride—help sustain your focus on long-term goals. Negative feelings frequently derail progress by triggering you to give up or avoid certain situations. Counter this frustration proactively. Channel your confidence by appreciating small daily efforts and gradual improvement. Write gratitude lists that recognize essential contributors behind the scenes.

Staying Driven

Revisit important ambitions by using visual reminders and accountability partners. Mark incremental achievements rather than just endpoints. Balance effort with rest to prevent burnout. Break intimidating ambitions into smaller milestones to steadily build momentum. Outline daily and weekly objectives to maintain clarity on what you need to do next.

Learn From Mistakes

When you fall short, avoid criticism that further sinks your motivation. Instead, practice self-compassion. Reevaluate your goals realistically, then renew your commitments and turn obstacles into opportunities. Even temporary setbacks carry lessons if you examine them constructively.

DEVELOPING EMPATHY

People skills matter as much as smarts for happiness and success. Emotional intelligence allows us to understand ourselves and others deeply. This empowers better communication and less conflict. To increase your empathy, you can:

- Learn to sense unspoken feelings.
- Respond with compassion, not impatience.
- Set your ego aside.
- Listen to connect on a human level.
- See from other people's perspectives.
- Discover people's inner light.
- Practice self-awareness.
- Ask yourself why you react in certain ways. What triggers your overreaction?
- Breathe instead of shouting when mad.
- Act, don't blame.
- Foster good vibes despite any stress.
- Grow emotional skills little by little, just like physical muscles.
- Catch mistaken judgments about others and try to imagine walking in their shoes.
- Ask questions, don't assume.

When people feel truly seen, walls between us crumble. Judging minds are quiet, and caring hearts are open.

Empathy Versus Sympathy

Empathy means deeply understanding how others feel and seeing things from their perspective. Sympathy just feels sorry for their troubles without as much emotional connection. Go beyond pity into truly imagining walking life in their shoes. How would daily hurdles feel physically, mentally, and spiritually? What memories and dreams stir for them? Thinking about others in this way helps you understand them on a deeper level.

Empathy Builds Connections

Empathy helps people in all types of relationships feel truly supported during good and bad times. Feelings go beyond words when people sense you intrinsically identify with them. Empathy fosters safe vulnerability and enables more authentic relating. Where egos once clashed, the connection can flow through gates of mutual understanding.

Leading With Empathy

Great leaders uplift teams by compassionately acknowledging the reality and aspirations of others. This inspires commitment, not coerced obedience. True leadership stems from serving others, not glorifying personal acclaim.

Progress follows moving souls, not just situations. Seek understanding before you seek to be understood. Meet confusion with patience. Lean into tensions with curiosity to help diffuse tension.

Showing Empathy

We all face loss, fear, and anger. Yet, people still remember small acts of unexpected kindness years later, easing the pain in hard moments. Tell stories that spread hope and show up for people. Volunteer at support groups. Help struggling neighbors with yard work. Teach the young. These are all ways you can show your empathy.

Practice Feeling Emotions

To practice feeling different emotions, act out made-up scenes as different troubled characters. Keep in my that good listeners respond with empathy questions, not quick fixes. Explore different perspectives. The distress people feel often makes sense given their history and dreams. Resist judging failures. Instead, imagine walking years in their shoes.

Setting Emotional Boundaries

Hold hope consistently for people while accepting what's beyond your control. Your care cannot eliminate the struggles of other people. Support them to play an active role in bettering the situation realistically and gradually. Manage your expectations. Maintain your self-care habits, so you can stabilize your emotional reservoir. Monitor compassion fatigue if you are overwhelmed by a situation.

Empathy Resolves Conflicts

Listen for unspoken worries that create arguments. Name the elephant in the room gently, then brainstorm ways to address the issue, making both parties okay. Build agreement first, validating positions before problem-solving tensions. Even the most furious attacks signal underlying wounds. Where open ears outmatch mouths, walls crumble, and humanity is found.

Digital Empathy Challenges

Online debates often demonize dissenters and spread hate. Comments that counter crude attacks with curiosity can sometimes help humanize nasty exchanges. However, you may need to opt out entirely rather than risk harm. Promote media literacy. We must lead technology morally, not be led by it.

Growing Empathy Expertise: Reading Body Language

People's facial cues and posture can reveal hidden feelings. Rapid blinking signals anxiety. Crossed arms show discomfort. Match people's expressions and energy levels to relay care. Pay attention to nonverbal communication techniques. Try to notice how micro-shifts can subtly show unease.

Emotions Spread

People unconsciously "catch" moods from others near them. So, staying positive uplifts everyone's spirits during tense times. Share hope through humor cautiously. Fear also spreads quickly without vigilance. Emote encouragement through affirmative nodding, smiling, and connected eye contact. Avoid distraction when listening fully. Your environment influences your mindset, so infuse your surroundings with inspiration.

Listen More Than You Speak

When you impatiently problem-solve too soon, it blocks deeper sharing. Compassion comes through being curious. Solutions blossom once hurt embraces the light. Listen without time pressure or personal agenda. Those who trust you will unpack their complexity once they feel safe. Your calm presence can heal.

EMOTIONAL INTELLIGENCE IN SOCIAL SETTINGS

EI Builds Friendships

Listen closely so you can sense the emotional frequency of your friends. Try to name feelings directly to show care and interest. Don't invalidate what's challenging others. Avoid "fixing" through and practice empathy instead.

Love Depends on EI

Self-awareness prevents destructive dating habits by helping you manage your anxiety before subconsciously sabotaging promising connections through neediness or coldness. Conflict resolution uplifts partnerships by prioritizing mutual uplift over winning arguments. Romantic love thrives through empathic nurturing.

Emotional intelligence is important in all types of relationships, from casual to close connections. It helps prevent conflicts. It also helps resolve conflicts when they happen, as misunderstandings are bound to occur between people. We all need patience and grace with one another, and no one is perfect. Applied carefully over time, emotional intelligence can heal damaged relationships.

Growing Emotionally: Reflect on Progress

Consider who you were a few years ago. How have you grown wiser in managing anger or hurt? Do you understand people better today? Setbacks still happen, but focus on the effort you have made. Patience pays off.

Lifelong Benefits

Emotional skills grant relationship richness, resilience during hardship, and leadership gravitas earned through lived experience. Studies confirm that high EQ protects your mental and physical health.

Set Growth Goals

Establish goals to increase your patience, improve your focus when others speak, or engage in more positive self-talk to counter anxiety. Record your progress in a journal and notice small wins and insights over time to help maintain motivation. We all struggle sometimes. It's the journey that matters.

CASE STUDY: TURNING CONFLICT INTO CONNECTION

Escalating tensions erupted at Eastside High between students divided along socioeconomic lines, and inflammatory online posts fueled the fire. Previously minor slights in that hallways began escalating into vandalism after hours.

The principal, Ms. Hayes, responded first through a stern statement warning punishment for future misconduct, but the tensions continued. One student, Mariana, decided to host a listening circle to address root causes respectfully before the cycle of blame worsened.

Students shared their unacknowledged pain and hope. New policies arose, affirming all student perspectives. Mariana's student organization started hosting cross-cultural sports leagues, potlucks, and volunteer initiatives. This helped to uphold friendships through story-sharing. Even reluctant participants softened gradually.

As Mariana demonstrated, emotional intelligence uplifts communities through courageous vulnerability that can transform long-held assumptions. Both individual and collective growth unfolds when diverse voices speak candidly in wise spaces. Where there is division, caring persistence reveals humanity.

WRAPPING UP...

As Mariana demonstrated through mediation leadership, empathy proves profoundly relevant, not only individually elevating self-conduct but also unlocking collective advancement.

In increasingly pluralistic societies, cross-cultural rapport depends upon compassionately validating unique backgrounds and anchoring shared hopes. The pages ahead reveal timeless insights on fostering intercultural fluency through curiosity, wisdom, and courage to truly know diverse neighbors whose perspectives may seem initially foreign, yet whose hearts are undoubtedly familiar.

9
LEADING AND INFLUENCING PEERS

When the captain of the math club had to drop out halfway through competition season, a freshman named Lee suddenly found himself heading the struggling team. He remembered a quote his mentor shared with him by Simon Sinek, "Leadership is not about being in charge, it is about taking care of those in your charge." Lee studied techniques for motivating teammates, building trust, and resolving tensions. His caring leadership uplifted the squad's morale and scores. They ended up advancing impressively at regionals despite inauspicious beginnings, surprising even themselves through committed collaboration focused on service over ego.

Formal authority matters far less than wisdom and integrity for progress. Let's look at how everyday people can spark change by understanding opponents, empowering the marginalized, and guiding groups respectfully toward justice. We can advance through moral creativity that breaks the constraints of narrow worldviews.

THE ESSENCE OF PEER LEADERSHIP

Leadership emerges informally through those daring to guide teams, mentor newcomers, or challenge bias by example. This section will illustrate how peer influence can uplift communities without the need for power scepters but through earning respect, building trust, and stirring participation into purpose.

You'll learn to recognize the traits of a true leader. Support flows from inspiration, not edict. You'll learn to assess your potential to help people through large and small difficulties. Growth unfolds by focusing outwards, spending more energy listening than talking, framing dilemmas with collective wisdom, and celebrating tiny victories that widen capacity.

When doors close, young change-makers can rediscover openings. Limitations dissolve when met with care, creativity, and conviction. Where there are misunderstandings, we can mend tears with truth and care.

You can gain influence by helping teams, mentoring newcomers, and promoting inclusive norms through your example. Offer kind words when peers struggle. Check on isolated schoolmates compassionately. Suggest collaborative solutions during group conflicts. Appreciate people's efforts and gifts even through imperfect attempts. Uplift spirits and cumulative belonging by leading through care.

Great Leaders Serve

Wisdom earns respect more than ego or power. You can discern true leaders by their integrity when no one watches except their conscience. Do they act nobly or bend morals? As a leader, you must model dignity and poise, maintaining stability amidst surrounding chaos. Meet confusion with patience and meet fear with love. Imagine that every interaction is an opportunity to uplift people and expectations.

Bosses demand obedience by threats and rewards. Leaders inspire support through earned authority and empowering people. Forced compliance lacks soul and staying power.

Assess Your Potential

Reflect on your values, seek candid feedback, and watch for opportunities to help. Growth unfolds by focusing outward. You can practice daily by making small choices—whether it's defusing classroom cliques, challenging bigoted remarks, or championing community needs. Take stock of your talents that can make a difference and make note of any personal weaknesses that you need to improve on. At times, we all struggle to practice idealistic leadership with compassion. It's the continual commitment that matters most. Stay patient with yourself and others.

Find Youth Role Models

Selfless young champions like Malala Yousafzai can motivate your best self. Read biographies of heroes, then find similar mentors. Believe that your compassionate voice can uplift world views. Seek experienced coaches who can help you uphold your values. There will come times when you won't want to stay silent. Stand tall and speak gently, upholding what is right. Stay true. You will inspire far beyond eyes seen when courage leads.

GROW YOUR LEADERSHIP ABILITIES WITH COMMUNICATION

Influence requires clarity to connect authentically and cross-culturally. Frame requests and feedback thoughtfully understanding the values of your audience. Model the respect you want to see from members. Your vocal tone establishes your presence—speak assuredly yet gently. Propel your ideas into action by storytelling to ignite imaginations toward purposeful collaboration. Work to master communication skills across both interpersonal mediums, including one-on-one dialogue and mass mediums like public speeches. Learn how to start productive, networked conversations while also being able to deliver eloquent, impactful speeches. Become a Chief Listening Officer rather than only an impassioned mouthpiece. Talk little at first and listen much more than most.

Guide Decisions

Pose dilemmas through frameworks that elicit wisdom from groups before you evaluate alternatives. Weigh both logical and emotional impacts holistically. Express steady presence amidst any turmoil, focusing on constructive progress. Gather broad input respectfully, giving credence to lived experience, not just lofty theories. Synthesize viewpoints into limited key suggestions.

Share Your Vision

Stir passive participation into active commitment by helping your peers recognize personal stakes in community betterment. Vivid visions enliven everyone's goals. Help write participants into your narrative as integral changemakers. Channel passion through imagery and metaphor, painting pictures of alternatives beyond perceived constraints. Celebrate incremental victories toward milestones to demonstrate expanded capacity despite the odds.

Practice Daily

Request candid feedback after exchanges. How did your body language and diction project authority and empathy? Journal takeaways from conflicts and proposals. Note how disciplined thinkers promote solutions. Mentally compose intervention messaging as world events unfold. Set regular public speaking and listening comprehension goals to apply your leadership skills. After all, we grow through continual engagement, not innate abilities alone. We make progress by practicing principles consistently in both large and small interactions. Train your skills to strengthen your emotional regulation, stress management, and sensitivity to social dynamics.

When doors close, open windows for the communities that are awaiting your voice to channel undercurrents into purposeful waters that flow freely forward. Lead beyond the surface ripples to deeper connecting tributaries. Limitations dissolve when you administer sufficient care, creativity, and courage.

Responsibility and Accountability

Welcome obligations that uphold order, further goals, and empower members constructively. Consider the needs of both current and future generations impacted by policies.

Accept fair critique from others. Ask for the reasons behind both accomplishment lulls and conflicts. Leadership involves more listening, self-correction, and consensus-building than lecturing status claims. Make sure to model this accountability first.

Celebrate personal milestones and show your fun side while maintaining sufficient professionalism. Take time to master warm versus cool composure while staying genuine. Friendliness strengthens your visionary influence, yet authority requires impartial distance to uphold group integrity over personal loyalties.

Take time to recall reversals and project failures. Were there prevention opportunities you may have missed? How will you preemptively address such issues moving forward? Being able to constructively self-critique indicates true growth.

Through trial and triumph, we can better our communities together. Stay persistent and envision future freedoms made possible by sacrifices today. Where there is a need, meet it unflinchingly.

LEADING WITHOUT AUTHORITY

You can guide teams or groups and spark change without a formal title, and you can earn influence by solving problems with care, not ego. Uplift communities quietly through wisdom rather than acclaim or popularity.

You can learn to strengthen your suggestions by doing thorough research first. Understand group motivations so you can frame your appeals effectively. Build trust slowly by consistently delivering on your commitments, however small. Bring disagreeing voices together into consensus decisions around common hopes. Carefully attune yourself to subtle divisions that complicate group unity.

With commitment, unseen growth opportunities will arise from initial resistance. Destiny comes unexpectedly when persistence and courage guide teams toward undiscovered potential. Limitations that many perceived as permanent can dissolve when compassionately addressed through moral creativity beyond self-concern.

Lead humbly yet potently without needing permission. Fan sparks where resignation looms. Progress comes when you take persistent care to repeatedly confront constraints, opening up new channels quietly. You can irreversibly transform communities that were once separated.

Guide Peers Behind the Scenes

Earn influence by solving problems using your expertise and relationships without ego. Research issues thoroughly, then frame helpful suggestions that can help orient group values such as excellence and purpose. Quietly uplift communities through wisdom rather than acclaim. Model integrity consistently, uplift the underdogs, and challenge biases bravely yet gently. Progress follows conscience, not personal glory. Power flows through principle, patience, and care.

Use Personal Strengths

Strengthen your proposals through logic, visual impact, and rapport with group members. Compassionately lead by helping disagreeing voices to address their shared motivations. Do your best to craft compromises. Establish clarity around decision drivers—does the greatest good prioritize social equity? What trade-offs emerge? Incorporate dissenting voices while focusing on achievable mutual gains.

Model Initiative

As a peer partner, assess any group dilemmas, then respectfully recommend solutions that address the core worries and hopes. Publicly follow through on your commitments to reinforce momentum. Display integrity through unassuming support that steadily betters your environment. Consistency earns trust. Systems improve gradually as people accept evolving.

Navigate Group Dynamics

Pay attention to any interpersonal factions that may complicate consensus. Adapt your messaging to address diverse appeals. Facilitate graceful debates but uphold order. Identify shared interests that can unify conflicts into teams that are focused on goals. Community emerges through this kind of principled mediation, not domination. Promote psychological safety and allow introverts equal air time. Leaders should listen more than they speak. Guide differences into exchanges that rely on wisdom to broaden vantage points.

Work to establish safe circles for vulnerable discussions. Feature members who manage successful projects and spotlight the strategies they use. Leadership helps to develop strengths that can be applied to solving institutional challenges. Mastering these group skills can prepare you for advocacy in the future.

SUSTAINING LEADERSHIP

Outline five- to ten-year targets that track back to inspiring visions. Break these targets into milestones with review systems to adapt as unexpected situations come up. Envision a greater future that justifies making sacrifices today. Rally your groups around bold, measurable objectives that are scaled to be ambitious and require unified efforts.

Plan for Successors

Take the time to study institutions that successfully maintained excellence over time despite leadership changes. When you are ready to move on, select successors early and train them thoroughly to perpetuate the key values and momentum you have established. You can pass the torch smoothly and minimize setbacks by planning for transitions. Study historical writings that detail succession dynamics to maintain vision continuity and stabilize the group around uncertain leadership transitions over time and turbulence.

Reflect on Growth

Request candid assessments from supporters and neutral advisors on your strengths and mental blind spots. Use a journal to review past decision dynamics and note areas where you can improve. Examine your speech and actions accurately to refine the foundations of your integrity. Allowing self-awareness to mature lifts leaders beyond past troubles into wisdom that can protect others in the future.

Learn Tirelessly

Take in all the books, courses, and films you can to expand your strategic abilities for upcoming needs beyond your current responsibilities. Pursue lifelong learning intrinsically without ego. Exchange ideas with other teens, teachers, and leaders. The wise will always uplift more learners.

CASE STUDY: SANJANA

Sanjana noticed that there were struggling newcomers at her high school who lacked English fluency and cultural familiarity. These students often faced exclusion and sat alone during lunch breaks. The teacher advisors and counseling staff were overloaded with their existing cases. So, Sanjana independently created orientation mentorships to pair immigrant students with volunteers to assist in classroom basics and networking with peers.

Initial participants reported greatly reduced anxiety because they came to know at least one person at the school. Word spread. Sanjana's small initiative grew, welcoming thousands across greater metro regions by collaborating with nonprofits to scale the infrastructure, secure grants, and systematize the training programs. The program cultivated compassionate leadership abilities to teach active listening, nonviolent dialogue, and reconciliation capacities to strengthen communities holistically.

Sanjana demonstrated peer leadership's potential to dissolve barriers through persistent care. She was able to awaken belonging and possibility where isolation paralysis previously loomed. Her story shows us how progress unfolds through those daring to stand up, speak truths firmly yet gently, and walk alongside struggling neighbors.

WRAPPING UP...

Leading peers means committing to a growth journey that drives positive change. Start small by supporting struggling individuals around you. Build toward tackling bigger community issues later through collaboration.

In a globalized world, developing this adaptive leadership prepares for cooperation across nations, aiding those in need near and far. Even faraway challenges share common threads of isolation, hardship, and marginalization. Lead first to understand cultural nuance, but meet all with compassion. Stories and statistics may differ, but humanity endures. Where you find darkness, kindle light.

10

NAVIGATING LOVE AND ROMANTIC RELATIONSHIPS

"Love is not about how much you say 'I love you,' but how much you can prove that it's true."

— UNKNOWN

Ah, to be young and in love! Do you remember when you first noticed your crush start to glance your way across the cafeteria or hallway? Those fireworks that went off inside at the possibility they might actually like you back?

Ellie still smiles thinking about exchanging songs with her middle school sweetheart Nick through that era's version of Spotify playlists. The thrills and flutters of budding romance hold an undeniable magic.

Yet, we all know infatuation's honeymoon period eventually fades. Building truly meaningful connections requires nurturing bonds through ongoing understanding, care, and commitment.

This chapter explores how to navigate the landscape of teen dating, love, and relationships with wisdom. We'll cover laying the foundations of trust and communication, handling conflict gracefully, coping with breakups, and more.

While connections can unlock some of life's sweetest joys, they can also sometimes bring pain when struggling through hard times side-by-side. Learning relationship skills now will pay dividends for decades down the road.

So, buckle up for a thrilling ride through love's soaring highs and vexing lows. By keeping one eye on your commitments to personal growth alongside relationships, you'll flourish beautifully through life's adventures—solo or coupled.

UNDERSTANDING ROMANTIC FEELINGS

Embarking on romantic relationships is an exciting new adventure in your teen years. As you navigate these uncharted waters, having some guidance on what to expect can make the journey a bit smoother.

This section explores the natural process of emerging romantic feelings, the difference between crushes and deeper bonds, and setting healthy expectations for relationships. While the emotions of attraction can be exhilarating, they also often feel confusing and overwhelming at first. That's completely normal. By better understanding the psychological and biological factors behind your changing dynamic with others during adolescence, you'll be well-equipped to handle both the ups and downs.

There are so many wonderful discoveries ahead, including connecting meaningfully with someone special, falling in love, and continuing to unfold layers of your unique self in harmony with another. We'll guide you joyfully on this thrill ride called romance, belts fastened and hands in the air. Getting in tune with your authentic desires while respecting your own pace and boundaries allows healthy bonds to blossom in their own time.

The Biology of Attraction

During puberty, your body starts producing new hormones that drive both physical and romantic attraction. It's Mother Nature's way of getting you ready for adulthood.

Estrogen and testosterone, which increase during the teen years, are behind your changing chemistry. They create those intense "crush" feelings, fluttery butterflies in the stomach, and constant thoughts about someone. Basically, your hormones can make you a little love crazy.

Attraction also involves the brain's limbic system, which controls emotion. Seeing someone you like activates the "feel-good" dopamine and oxytocin. No wonder it makes you so happy. But too much dopamine can also lead to risky or obsessive behaviors— something for you to be aware of.

Understanding the difference between lust, passion, and real connection can help navigate relationships:

- Lust: A shallow physical desire for someone based mostly on attraction or infatuation. It's easy to confuse with love!
- Infatuation: An intense but usually short-lived passion or romantic feeling for someone. It can feel like an obsession.

- Love: A meaningful, lasting bond built over time through care, closeness, and commitment. It is the deepest form of connection with another person.

Managing intense emotions that come with attraction gets easier with practice. Being self-aware, communicating boundaries, and making wise choices will serve you well on your journey to healthy, meaningful relationships.

Crushes Versus Serious Relationships

Crushes, we all get them. A crush is an intense but usually temporary feeling of attraction to someone. You might obsessively think about them, get nervous or giddy when they're around, and want to be close to them.

Crushes are fun fantasies, but they're often based mostly on appearance, projected ideals, or chemistry rather than actual compatibility. Sometimes, crushes pass as quickly as they come on. Other times, they can slowly grow into something more.

If you continue getting to know your crush over time and move from surface-level connections to deeper intimacy, then a real friendship or relationship can develop. This includes truly seeing someone for who they are, caring deeply about them as a person, sharing your authentic self, growing in commitment, and choosing to build a bond not just based on looks or lust.

As an intense crush evolves into possible love, continuing to define and communicate your boundaries is key. Going from friends to romantic partners is a transition to navigate thoughtfully and is best done with openness, patience, and respect for what each person feels ready or not ready for.

If your feelings end up one-sided, don't despair. We've all been there. Refocus on self-care practices that build confidence from the inside out. Foster positive connections of all kinds with others. In time, remember there is a lid for every pot. When you're ready, be open to new people and experiences that await.

Healthy Expectations

It's easy to have unrealistic views of what romance should be like, especially with so many over-the-top media portrayals out there. Remind yourself that what you see on TV, movies, or social media is heavily glamorized! No couple is perfectly happy 24-7.

As a teen, rather than expecting a fairy tale, focus on positive relationship building blocks, such as honest communication, respect, trust, embracing imperfections, shared interests, laughter, and comfortable silences. Base connections first on friendship before romance.

Believe you are worthy of love just as you are. If you struggle with self-esteem or confidence, this can negatively impact relationships. Work on self-care and get support if you don't feel "enough." You deserve to both give and receive care.

All couples argue or disagree sometimes, that's normal and healthy. However, avoid name-calling, accusations, or storms of drama. Successfully solve conflicts through compromises, taking space if needed, and non-violent communication.

While coupling up is exciting, don't forget the importance of nurturing your individuality too. Keep seeing friends and pursuing personal goals and hobbies. Trust and healthy attachment grow when you maintain some independence.

Stay open-minded, keep expectations realistic, and don't rush things too fast physically or emotionally, and relationships will have room to blossom beautifully.

Ellie thinks back fondly on her early relationship with Nick as a great example of some positive foundations. Even in middle school, they focused first on building a solid friendship before rushing into romance. A shared love of music was their common ground.

Laughter came easy for them, Nick was always making Ellie crack up with silly jokes. When occasional misunderstandings happened, they talked them out openly and honestly, with no drama or accusations.

Though their youthful bond didn't end up lasting through high school, Ellie appreciated how Nick enabled her to feel comfortable being imperfect around him. She never felt pressured to be someone else. Their attachment grew in trust and respect by embracing each other's quirks.

While exciting to couple up, Ellie made sure to still pursue individual friendships, hobbies, and goals, too. Nick supported her dreams. In the end, she now sees their innocent eighth-grade love as a wonderful foundation for healthy relationships moving forward.

BUILDING AND MAINTAINING RELATIONSHIPS

Once that initial spark of chemistry and attraction leads you to start dating someone, you'll both discover there's so much more to learn about each other as you build a relationship over time. Nurturing bonds requires some effort, it's a skill set to develop together.

This section outlines key elements like communication, trust, and respect that form the foundation for healthy, thriving connections.

We'll explore how to compassionately discuss your inner worlds, resolve conflicts, establish boundaries, and support each other's growth.

Creating true intimacy goes beyond physical closeness to include emotional and mental openness. This gradual vulnerability awakens the amazing experience of being fully seen, known, and cared for by someone special and getting to know them deeply in return.

Along the journey, challenges will arise as you mesh two unique personalities and sets of needs. But armed with the relationship tools here, you'll be equipped to navigate issues skillfully as you learn and mature together.

If you give your spark the right care, attention, and oxygen, it has the potential to grow into a steady flame of reciprocal love, care, and understanding that can light up your life.

Communication in Relationships

Being able to talk openly and honestly with your partner is key to a healthy relationship. Discuss your thoughts and feelings regularly so you both understand each other better. This includes clarifying wants/needs around physical intimacy so you're on the same page about consent and are comfortable progressing one step at a time.

If conflicts come up, address issues calmly at a time when you're both relaxed and not heated in the moment. Listen, validate, and compromise rather than attack. Misunderstandings happen, so talk them through. Bring a spirit of patience, care, and willingness to understand tough talks.

Digital communication can connect you instantly but also lead to confusion if you misread texts or social media posts. Balance virtual interactions with regular in-person ones to build deeper bonds. Keep communication frequent, thoughtful, and positive.

Trust and Respect

Trust forms the bedrock of a healthy relationship. Build it by being reliable and accountable. If you say you'll do something, follow through. Open up gradually about your feelings, background, and fears—we all have our stories. Mutual vulnerability strengthens bonds over time.

Respect your partner's boundaries and need for personal time and space away from you. Encourage, praise honesty, and avoid harsh criticisms. In arguments, stick to resolving the issue rather than aiming attacks at one another. Follow the Golden Rule: Treat your partner as you want to be treated.

Navigating Boundaries

Having strong personal boundaries means knowing your limits and values. Communicate yours clearly to avoid getting pressured into situations you don't want. It's okay to say no, even if it's uncomfortable.

Likewise, carefully listen if your partner shares their boundaries and respect them fully. Compromise when needed, but never coerce or shame. Make consent, comfort, and safety top priorities as you navigate physical intimacy together one step at a time.

Stay confident in the face of peer pressure. Draw strength from those who build you up rather than tear you down. Surround yourself with supportive friends as you grow into the person you want to be.

THE CHALLENGES OF TEEN RELATIONSHIPS

Along with all the fun of new love and connections comes some tricky terrain to navigate. Relationships can hit rough patches, and sometimes come to a sad end. Teens also face unique situations like long-distance bonds or meeting partners online.

This section explores how to gracefully handle common relationship challenges. You'll learn positive coping strategies for painful breakups and transitioning to new chapters. We'll share creative ideas for keeping intimacy thriving across miles and getting to know online-only loves safely.

Finally, we'll delve into balancing your individual life dreams with coupledom. The two don't have to be mutually exclusive! With some self-awareness and ongoing communication, relationships can absolutely support both partners' goals rather than forcing anyone to conform.

There will be moments of turbulence on this relational flight, with some expected ups and downs. But equipped with these tips, you'll sail smoothly through the stormiest patches. Steady as you grow, centered within your most authentic self as you navigate all of love's mysteries and adventures together

Dealing With Breakups

Breakups can bring intense and overpowering emotions. Allow yourself to fully feel and process the grief, pain, anger, or loneliness rather than bottling it up. Reach out to connect with close friends who will listen and comfort without judgment. Pour your feelings into music, poetry, or a journal. In time, these self-care practices help lift sadness so you can start moving forward again one baby step at a time.

In reflecting on what you've learned from the relationship and breakup, forgive yourself *and* your ex for mistakes made along the way. You're both growing and learning. In future bonds, apply lessons drawn from this experience to build on—two steps forward for every step back!

There's no perfect formula for when to start dating again but focus first on nurturing inner wisdom, confidence, and worth. Embrace activities that reignite your unique sparks and passions. When you feel centered in a place of contentment within yourself instead of seeking it externally, you know you're ready for whatever positive connections and adventures await around the next bend.

Long Distance and Online Relationships

Long-distance relationships (LDRs) have ups and downs. Finding creative ways to connect besides just texting helps nurture intimacy that goes deeper than physical. Openly communicate your needs, schedule regular virtual date nights, play online games together, mail each other care packages, make handwritten letters and playlist mixtapes to share your inner worlds.

If cultivating an online-only bond with someone, proceed slowly and with care before bringing it into "real life." Not everyone presents authenticity honestly online at first. Watch for inconsistent facts, excuses to meet up or video chat, or requests for excessive favors or money early on as possible warning signs of lies, manipulation, or abuse, aka "catfishing." Verify details and listen to your intuition. You deserve genuine care and connection, don't ever compromise personal safety or boundaries.

Love and Future Planning

The exhilarating feelings that come with falling for someone can be all-consuming, making it tempting to abandon individual dreams to dive into Couple Land forever. Yet the healthiest partners empower each other's hopes rather than limiting them. Openly communicate your unfolding career plans, college goals, and bucket list dreams with one another as you navigate the next chapters. True love supports growth; it doesn't demand anyone to dim their own lights! Stay anchored in self-awareness and tend lovingly to your passions. Wherever your journey leads, you'll glow radiantly together or independently.

CASE STUDY: SARAH AND KATE

Sarah and Kate became fast friends when they met in eighth-grade art class. What started as chatting over sketchbooks quickly grew into sleepovers, inside jokes, and heart-to-heart talks about life. They loved exploring new vegan cafes and thrift shops together while bonding through music and creativity.

When they reached sophomore year, new emotions entered the picture. Sarah developed an instant connection with Liam, a guitarist in the school jazz band. As she fell into the bliss bubble of first love, less time was left for BFF dates with Kate. More and more, Kate felt herself struggling for Sarah's attention against her new boyfriend.

Liam consumed Sarah's thoughts 24-7. Her texts to Kate became infrequent one-word responses. Often she'd forget plans they'd made together. When Kate tried to open up about feeling hurt, Sarah brushed it off, saying she was just "going through a phase" and that Kate didn't understand because she'd never been in love.

After a blow-up fight about broken promises, the childhood friend-ship faded, leaving Kate feeling abandoned and betrayed. Sarah got so wrapped up in her relationship that she lost sight of nurturing other bonds that once mattered so much.

The passion of romance can be intoxicating, but frequently burns bright and fast. Lasting love requires maintaining balance among all relationships—especially with those who loved you first. Through open communication and emotional maturity, Sarah hopes to rebuild burnt bridges and integrate both friendships and romantic partners into her life in a healthier way.

WRAPPING UP...

As we conclude this chapter, reflect on all that you've learned about navigating the exciting world of romance, love, and relationships. While the thrill of forging new bonds can be intoxicating, also remember that not every attraction or situation is meant to last.

Whether flirtations stay surface-level crushes or blossom into deeper lifelong connections, these experiences will undoubtedly expand your understanding of yourself and others. The growth that comes from riding both the highs and lows serves to develop emotional intelligence and maturity.

As you leave your teen years behind and enter young adulthood, applying these relationship skills will enable you to show up fully and communicate authentically. You'll be able to set healthy boundaries, resolve conflicts, and nurture trust and equality with partners.

Most importantly, maintain confidence in your self-worth throughout it all and stay anchored from within rather than seeking validation solely from external bonds. Honor your unique goals and passions. Choose partnerships that support your highest growth, not limit it.

Now, equipped with all of the social strategies and knowledge gathered in this book, you have a solid game plan for interpersonal success! Next, we'll tie everything together into an actionable road map for building confidence, connection, and community wherever life takes you...

The skills to gracefully give and receive care in relationships, through both words and actions, will serve you well at every age and stage. This emotional awareness and wisdom will blossom into an ever-growing garden, one we hope brings you and your loved ones much joy and nourishment for years to come.

Thinking back to our old friends Nick and Ellie, that young couple we met at the start of the chapter exchanging songs and crushes— did their budding middle school romance last?

While their puppy love connection faded as high school priorities and social circles shifted, the positive building blocks they practiced —then trust, laughter, and compromise—became the foundation for relationships later on.

Even though their adolescent bond only spanned eighth-grade carpools and hallway hand-holds, their communication abilities and willingness to embrace imperfections endured.

Ellie reflects now with gratitude at how Nick helped awaken early romantic stirrings with patience and respect. In college, new dating adventures called back memories of that gentle boy who made mix CDs overflowing with shy affection.

So, as you grow into adulthood, know that every interaction offers opportunities to hone interpersonal tools for future happiness, no matter how fleeting. Let the laughter, trust, and communication flow!

KEEPING THE GAME ALIVE

Now that you're equipped with superpowers of social smarts, unshakable confidence, deep friendships, and much more, it's your turn to light the torch for others.

By sharing your true thoughts about this book on Amazon, you're not just writing a review; you're guiding other teens to the treasure map of life skills they're searching for.

Your wisdom counts, your words matter. Help us keep the spirit of *Social Skills for Teens* glowing bright by passing on your insights.

A million thanks for joining this mission. The flame of *Social Skills for Teens* burns brighter with every story and experience shared – and you're a vital spark in this beautiful blaze.

Scan the QR code below

CONCLUSION

As we close this chapter exploring the world of social skills, I've so enjoyed getting to share this journey with you. Looking back on all we've covered, I hope you feel prepared now to navigate life's tricky social terrain with a bit more grace.

We started out discussing why people skills matter so much and how they empower us to show up as our best selves and make meaningful connections. Getting to know our unique gifts through practices like self-reflection makes it easier to relate to others more authentically. Communication tools like active listening help us understand different perspectives.

Building new relationships expands our community. Handling conflict and rejection isn't easy, but it builds resilience. Influencing and persuading others effectively is an art. And romance, while thrilling, requires nurturing bonds through care and commitment.

My wish is that you feel equipped now to handle all sorts of social situations and their messy complexities. But hey, we never stop learning—every new encounter offers opportunities to build trust, empathy, and wisdom if we stay open.

Wherever you want to keep developing abilities, small daily practice is key. Join a club, volunteer, role-play speeches, and make social media goals true to your values. When conflicts happen, reflect on how to respond better next time.

The seeds you plant now socially will blossom for years to come. What you've gained isn't just useful for the teen phase; they're life skills for adulthood, career success, relationships, and building community.

I'm reminded of Bryan Stevenson's journey of developing extraordinary communication talents through his legal advocacy, leading with empathy, and empowering others. Wherever you feel passion, use it to lift people.

My hope is we've started ripples of positive change in how we all relate. The world needs more everyday ambassadors spreading compassion. Our story continues as part of the broader human tale. Go write your next incredible chapter!

FINAL CASE STUDY: ALEXANDRA

As a shy eighth grader, Alexandra dreaded starting at a large public high school where she knew no one. She had struggled to make friends since elementary school, despite longing for real connections. Alexandra watched groups of laughing teens from the outskirts, wondering if she'd ever find her people.

During freshman year, she joined the anime club hoping to connect over shared interests. But Alexandra held back, uncertain how to insert herself into conversations. Her inability to speak up reinforced the belief she was unlikable.

After reading a book on social skills over summer break, Alexandra decided sophomore year would be different. She used self-assessment tools to better understand her introverted tendencies and how those shaped past social anxiety. Alexandra then set a goal to practice one new communication strategy a month, tracking her progress.

Small wins mounting slowly boosted Alexandra's confidence. She initiated conversations by asking peers about their favorite anime. Focusing outward rather than fearing judgment kept Alexandra grounded. By the second semester, acquaintances became lunch buddies. Bonding over funny memes and boba runs laid friendship foundations.

In junior year, Alexandra was elected anime club secretary. Organizing events forced her to pitch ideas assertively and delegate effectively. Her enthusiasm drew more students in. Alexandra also mentored new members, remembering how alone she once felt. After a gaming tournament fundraising win, the principal even asked her to join a student advisory panel to provide input on school policies based on Alexandra's proven leadership talents.

Now a senior, Alexandra is hosting Japanese culture immersion events bringing teens from rival schools together, too. No one can believe this is the same wallflower new girl from four years ago. By leaning into her unique personality and then honing her communication abilities, Alexandra stopped hiding her light. Her warm glow continues inspiring peers to embrace their inner shine as well.

SELF-REFLECTION AND EXERCISES

Welcome to a special section designed to help you apply and integrate the social skills you learned throughout the book. Experience shows we absorb information best when we actively engage with it. So, get ready to listen, observe, discuss, journal, role-play, and more.

Consider this a tool kit filled with hands-on ways to transform yourself and your relationships. I'll offer reflection prompts to increase self-awareness, plus exercises to practice new habits. You'll log interpersonal growth in action. My hope? These activities plant seeds for confidence, empathy, and wisdom lasting a lifetime.

Let's dive into the exercise and reflection questions below, exploring influences currently shaping your social landscape. Respond thoughtfully as we build muscles vital to navigating life ahead. With an openness to see yourself and others deeply, exciting discoveries await.

Introduction

Reflection: What social challenges or goals currently feel most pressing for you? How do you hope this book will help provide guidance?

Chapter 1

Exercise: Observe your social media feed today. Make notes about what norms, values, and unwritten rules seem important to that online community.

Reflection: What social hierarchies or cliques exist in your school or activities? How do you currently navigate them? Where do you see room to grow in standing up to negative peer pressure?

Chapter 2

Exercise: Use the self-assessment tools provided to better understand your personality, strengths, weaknesses, and emotional triggers.

Reflection: How might knowing yourself more deeply help you show up authentically and confidently in social situations?

Chapter 3

Exercise: Practice active listening with a friend. Reflect on how it felt to truly hear their perspective.

Reflection: What communication habits would you like to improve? Set one to two specific goals and track your progress.

Chapter 4

Exercise: Reach out to someone outside your normal social circle this week, asking thoughtful questions to understand their world.

Reflection: What new insight or connection did you gain from listening to their story?

Chapter 5

Exercise: Conduct an audit of your social media profiles. Are you conveying your values? Are any changes needed?

Reflection: How could you use your online presence more intentionally for self-expression versus peer validation?

Chapter 6

Exercise: Journal after your next conflict. What worked or didn't
work in your response? Any lessons for the future?

Reflection: How might seeing clashes as teaching moments help
you heal and grow?

Chapter 7

Exercise: Practice framing a request persuasively to friends or
family. What vocabulary and style worked effectively?

Reflection: Where could you use better influence skills to achieve
goals or stand up to peer pressure?

Chapter 8

Exercise: Next debate, consciously try to listen for feelings behind
the facts. Were you able to better understand all sides?

Reflection: How might leading with more empathy resolve conflicts
faster? What shifts might that require from you?

Chapter 9

Exercise: Take on a small leadership project organizing friends
around an idea you feel passionate about. What challenges and joys
did you experience while motivating them?

Reflection: How did putting service above ego lead to more unity? Where else might you apply collaborative leadership?

Chapter 10

Exercise: Discuss relationship red flags and boundaries openly with a friend. Did you gain any new perspective on unhealthy patterns?

Reflection: If your best friend were in this relationship situation, what advice would you give? Apply that same care to yourself.

Conclusion

Reflection: What have been your key takeaways from this social skills journey? How will you continue growing your abilities moving forward?

As we wrap up, I hope you feel empowered by having actively worked through the exercises and prompts over each chapter. Discussing key ideas, observing scenarios mindfully, rehearsing improved responses, and reflecting openly can train our interpersonal muscles like nothing else.

Remember that your learnings represent beginnings. Review your responses in future years—I suspect you'll smile at how far you've come. For now, integrate the most meaningful lessons into your daily life. Share these tools with friends who need them. Most importantly, continue your personal growth journey with compassion.

By engaging with rather than just absorbing information, you own these skills forever. Well done sticking with what was often challenging work. I have no doubt you'll continue blossoming into an ethical, socially intelligent leader who improves the lives of many.

REFERENCES

2016-2020 programs-Express yourself! (n.d.). Star Style Fadio. https://www.starstyleradio.com/copy-of-express-yourself-radio

A quote from How to Win Friends and Influence People. (n.d.). Goodreads. https://www.goodreads.com/quotes/1962-you-can-make-more-friends-in-two-months-by-becoming

Arthur, R. (n.d.). *How Stephen King almost threw away his most successful book.* Fully Booked. https://fully-booked.ca/editorials/stephen-king-carrie-almost-threw-away

Carmack, N. (2014, May 27). *Listen up! Keys to active listening.* BOS Staffing. https://www.bosstaff.com/2014/05/27/active_listening_skills

Cialdini, R. B. (2007). *Influence: The psychology of persuasion.* Collins.

Covey, S. (n.d.). *Culture of empathy builder: Stephen Covey.* Culture of Empathy. http://cultureofempathy.com/References/Experts/Stephen-Covey.htm

de Guzman, M. (2020). *2007.* Unl.edu. https://extensionpublications.unl.edu/assets/html/g1751/build/g1751.htm

deGrasse Tyson, N. (2001). *Coming to our Senses: Neil deGrasse Tyson.* Neil deGrasse Tyson. https://neildegrassetyson.com/essays/2001-03-coming-to-our-senses

Hearing what isn't said. (n.d.). Saint Martin's University. https://www.stmartin.edu/news-and-stories/stories/hearing-what-isnt-said

Jiménez-Picón, N., et al. (2021). The relationship between mindfulness and emotional intelligence as a protective factor for healthcare professionals: Systematic review. *International Journal of Environmental Research and Public Health, 18*(10), 5491. https://doi.org/10.3390/ijerph18105491

Love is not about how much you say "I love you," but how much you can prove that it's true. (2018, May 3). Steemit. https://steemit.com/love/@olsm/love-is-not-about-how-much-you-say-i-love-you-but-how-much-you-can-prove-that-it-s-true

Neil Postman: Children are the living messages we send to a time we will not see. (n.d.). Quotes. https://www.quotes.net/quote/53461

Riehm, K. E., et al. (2019). Associations between time spent using social media and internalizing and externalizing problems among U.S. youth. *JAMA Psychiatry, 76*(12), 1266–1273. https://doi.org/10.1001/jamapsychiatry.2019.2325

Sinek, S. (n.d.). *School leadership 2.0.* School Leadership 2.0. https://schoolleadership20.com

Solis, B. (2007, August 28). *Social media is about sociology, not technology.* Brian Solis. https://briansolis.com/2007/08/social-media-is-about-sociology-not-html

Top 2 Shubhankar Mishra quotes (2024 update) (n.d.). Quotefancy. https://quotefancy.
com/shubhankar-mishra-quotes

Umberson, D., & Karas Montez, J. (2011). Social relationships and health: A flash-
point for health policy. *Journal of Health and Social Behavior*, *51*(1), 54–66.
https://doi.org/10.1177/0022146510383501

www.ingramcontent.com/pod-product-compliance
Lightning Source LLC
Chambersburg PA
CBHW070712130626
46553CB00005B/1947